The Cheapskate's Guide to
SAN FRANCISCO

The Cheapskate's Guide to
SAN FRANCISCO

Where to Go, What to See, Where to Shop, Where to Stay— All on a Limited Budget

CONNIE EMERSON

A CITADEL PRESS BOOK
Published by Carol Publishing Group

A Citadel Press Book
Published by Carol Publishing Group
Citadel Press is a registered trademark of Carol Communications, Inc.

Editorial, sales and distribution, rights and permissions inquiries should be addressed to Carol Publishing Group, 120 Enterprise Avenue, Secaucus, N.J. 07094.

In Canada: Canadian Manda Group, One Atlantic Avenue, Suite 105, Toronto, Ontario M6K 3E7

Carol Publishing Group books may be purchased in bulk at special discounts for sales promotion, fund-raising, or educational purposes. Special editions can be created to specifications. For details, contact Special Sales Department, Carol Publishing Group, 120 Enterprise Avenue, Secaucus, N.J. 07094.

Manufactured in the United States of America

10 9 8 7 6 5 4 3 2 1

Library of Congress Cataloging-in-Publication Data

Emerson, Connie, 1930–
    The cheapskate's guide to San Francisco : where to go, what to see, where to shop, where to stay—all on a limited budget / by Connie Emerson.
        p. cm.
    "A Citadel Press book."—T.p. verso.
    ISBN 0–8065–1901–0
    1. San Francisco (Calif.)—Guidebooks. I. Title.
F869.S33E45 1997
917.94'610453—dc21   97–17781
                                                          CIP

Contents

Introduction

San Francisco. Journalist and TV personality Alistair Cooke has described it as "the most individual and engaging of American cities." Actress Julie Christie calls it "exciting, moody, exhilarating." Former president of France Georges Pompidou said, "Of all the cities in the United States, it is the one whose name, the world over, conjures up the most visions and more than any other incites one to dream."

But what is it that makes San Francisco so special?

As cities go, it isn't large. The population is listed as only 759,300, although San Francisco is the hub of the nation's fifth largest metropolitan area, with a population of about six million. More than sixteen million visitors arrive each year, most of whom wish they had planned to stay longer.

Built on forty-three hills and surrounded by water on three sides, San Francisco is a place of leafy lanes and panoramic views; of sailboats dotting the bay, with Marin County and East Bay greenery providing the backdrop. Sunday painters and sidewalk string quartets are part of the landscape. Dragons cavort through the streets of Chinatown during Chinese New Year and Italians play bocce ball on courts in adjacent North Beach.

In addition to the sights that are quintessentially San Francisco, The City has its own array of distinctive smells—of eucalyptus, fresh sea air, dried fish, and strong coffee; of night-blooming jasmine and newly mowed grass.

Its sounds are of bus brakes, cable car bells, boom boxes,

and street entertainers. And its spirit embraces a tolerance that accommodates alternate ways of life, foreign languages, and cultural differences with élan. In fact, San Francisco is perhaps the most ethnically diverse and lifestyle-tolerant city in the United States.

Of course, The City (the first letter of those two words are always capitalized) has its flaws. When the fog rolls in or the wind is off the water, San Francisco can be clammy and cold. On those rare days when the mercury soars above 90 degrees, tourists and residents alike swelter inside nonair-conditioned restaurants and shops. Parking is difficult, or at least expensive. As in all big cities, crime is a problem, and at times it seems that the homeless have taken over the sidewalks downtown.

Despite its flaws, San Francisco has a charisma you won't find anywhere else in America: flower stands brimming with daffodils, carnations, and roses; fog horns moaning and seagulls keening while The City sleeps under a gray blanket of fog; painted-lady Victorians and sleek chrome and glass skyscrapers; and an exotic ethnic mix—both of residents and tourists. All combine to provide enchantment and endless opportunities for entertainment.

Ever since its beginnings, San Francisco has been a fascinating place. In 1579, Sir Francis Drake landed north of San Francisco Bay and claimed the territory for England. Then, in 1769, the Franciscan padres under the leadership of Father Junipero Serra began establishing missions in Alta California along a 650-mile trail stretching from San Diego to Sonoma. One of them, Mission Dolores, was founded in 1776 on the western edge of what is now known as the Mission District.

Also in 1769, the Spanish explorer Gaspar De Portola led an expedition from Mexico to establish settlements in Upper California. Portola's party discovered San Francisco Bay on November 2 of that year.

The first European settlement on the site of the present city was established in 1776 by Spanish officer Colonel Juan

Bautista de Anza, who founded the Presidio on the southern shore of the entrance to San Francisco Bay. By 1835 the garrison had grown into the village of Yerba Buena, which was to remain its name until it was officially christened San Francisco in 1847.

In 1846, as a result of the Bear Flag Rebellion, California declared itself independent from Mexico. Two years later, with the signing of the Treaty of Guadaloupe-Hidalgo, which ended the Mexican-American War, it officially became a part of the United States. That same year, James Marshall discovered gold along the south fork of the American River in the Sierra foothills, and overnight San Francisco became a boomtown.

Tents and makeshift buildings served as boarding houses, laundries, brothels, and stores where miners' pickaxes, mules, and provisions were sold. Men who were reluctant to make the long trip overland across the United States boarded ships bound for Mexico, walked across the Isthmus of Tehuantepec, and sailed up the West Coast to San Francisco harbor. Also arriving in its ports were people of all colors, customs, and accents from countries around the world. And as each new wave of immigrants arrived, they established enclaves within San Francisco where life went on much as it had in the old country.

By 1849, merchants, miners, and adventurers, sometimes accompanied by their families, were arriving by the thousands at the jumping-off point for the Mother Lode. Some proceeded on to the foothills, hoping to strike it rich, while others decided that they had a better chance of achieving financial success by remaining in San Francisco and providing supplies and services.

Ten years later, with the discovery of the fabulous Comstock silver lode in western Nevada, San Francisco became even more prosperous. Merchants like Levi Strauss, bankers like Charles Crocker, and mine owners like William Sharon set up operations in Virginia City, but their wealth was funneled back to San Francisco, where they built mansions and set up additional business operations, or otherwise invested their funds.

At first, San Francisco, with its abundance of nouveau riche residents, aimed at sophistication but often fell short of the mark. By the time of the rebuilding after the disastrous earthquake of 1906, The City was well on its way to developing a sense of style. With each decade, the level of sophistication reached new heights. There was tea dancing at the Palace Court to the music of Anson Weeks; the symphony, opera, and ballet were on their way to becoming among America's finest. Department stores in the Union Square area could hold their own with any in the East, and charity balls were as gala as any you could find.

An economic power since gold rush days, San Francisco evolved into one of the country's great financial centers. It developed an intellectual side as well, with eight colleges and universities within the city limits and two world-class universities nearby—the University of California at Berkeley and Stanford University thirty-five miles down the Peninsula on the edge of Palo Alto. The arts flourished, in part because of San Franciscans' willingness to embrace new ideas. Today, San Francisco boasts the highest concentration of arts organizations in the nation.

Its naturally spectacular setting, enhanced by an exciting array of architectural styles, makes it one of the most magnificent of North American cities. When you approach San Francisco from the Golden Gate or Bay Bridge on a clear day, or when downtown comes into full view as you round the curve on U.S. Highway 101 from the south, The City is impossibly beautiful. Its predominantly white buildings glow in the sunlight as they cascade down the hillsides or rise up from the flatland in towers, spires, and even a pyramid to meet the cerulean sky.

It's easy to leave your heart in San Francisco. It's not so hard, either, to leave your wallet there. Hotel rates are among the highest in the nation. Meals at the top restaurants are as expensive as in Manhattan. The selection of luxury goods is worthy of the biggest of the big-time spenders. Nonetheless, San Francisco can be a bargain-lover's delight—which brings us to the purpose of this book. Each chapter, whether it focuses on accommodations, dining, shopping, or the other elements that go into a trip's success, is aimed at showing you how to get the most for your vacation dollar. We don't always highlight the least expensive choices, since paying very little and getting very little in exchange is not our idea of a bargain. What we do, instead, is concentrate on value received for money and time spent, because vacation days are often more precious than cash.

Since all travelers don't travel at the same pace or find joy in the same activities, we have tried to accommodate a variety of tastes and travel styles. The decisions about what to include are of necessity subjective. After all, books have a finite numbers of pages and it wouldn't be possible to list all of San Francisco's attractions or mention every one of its 3,300 restaurants, even if they merited the attention. We hope, however, that our choices will coincide with yours.

We also hope, after you visit The City by the Golden Gate, that you'll love San Francisco too, that you will realize it's a city like no other, and that you'll feel like legendary newspaper columnist Herb Caen felt when he wrote: "I hope I go to heaven, and when I do, I'm going to do what every San Franciscan does when he gets there,...He looks around and says, 'It ain't bad, but it ain't San Francisco.'"

The Cheapskate's Guide to
SAN FRANCISCO

CHAPTER

1

Pretrip Prep

It's great to take off on the spur of the moment, go somewhere you've always wanted to be—or see again. It's fairly impractical, though, when you want to maximize your travel time and money. You'll almost always get more value when you plan ahead. Phone calls made, letters or faxes sent, and a few hours spent in research can translate into hundreds of dollars of savings, even if you plan to stay in San Francisco only three or four days.

Savings Plan

Gather together all the information on San Francisco that you can find (see chapter 13 for where to find it). If you have limited time for research, concentrate on getting information on transportation and accommodations, because that's where your biggest savings can be made.

About fifty major scheduled airlines serve San Francisco International Airport (SFO). The major North American carriers include:

Air Canada	800/776-3000
Alaska Airlines	800/426-0333
American and American Eagle	800/433-7300
American West Airlines	800/235-9292
Canadian Airlines International	800/426-7000
Continental	800/525-0280

Delta Air Lines	800/221-1212
Frontier Airlines	800/432-1359
Hawaiian Airlines	800/367-5320
Midwest Express Airlines	800/452-2022
Northwest Airlines	800/225-2525
Shuttle by United	800/748-8853
Southwest Airlines	800/435-9792
Trans World Airlines	800/221-2000
United Airlines	800/241-6522
USAir	800/842-5374
Virgin Atlantic Airlines	800/862-8621

Among foreign airlines with flights to and from San Francisco International are:

Aeroflot	415/434-2300
Aerolineas Argentinas	800/333-0276
Air Afrique	800/456-9192
Air China	415/392-2156
Air France	800/237-2747
Air New Zealand	800/262-1234
Alitalia Airlines	800/233-5730
Asiana Airlines	800/227-4262
Avianca Airlines	800/284-2622
British Airways	800/247-9297
Cathay Pacific Airways	800/233-2742
China Airlines	800/227-5118
Egypt Air	415/928-1700
El Al Israel Airlines	800/223-6700
Emirates	800/777-3999
Finnair	800/950-5000
Iberia Airlines of Spain	800/772-4642
Japan Airlines	800/525-3663
KLM Royal Dutch Airlines	800/374-7747
Korean Air	415/956-6373
Lufthansa	800/645-3880
Mexicana	800/531-7921
Philippine Airlines	800/435-9725
Qantas Airways	800/227-4500

Sabena Belgian World Airlines	800/873-3900
Singapore Airlines	800/742-3333
South African Airlines	800/722-9675
Swissair	800/221-4750
Thai Airways International	800/426-5204
Varig Brazilian Airlines	800/468-2744

Whatever airline you fly, if you're savvy, you'll be paying less for your ticket than most of the people sitting around you. And you'll be sitting in an aisle seat instead of being squished in the middle.

Paying the least and getting the best happens only to those who plan ahead or are a lot luckier than most of us. By starting early, you can shop around for the best deals (or have a good travel agent do it for you). You have a good chance of getting an aisle or window seat when you check in early on the day of your flight, but your odds are even better when you arrange your seating in advance.

As with any destination, you're most apt to come up with the best airfares to San Francisco when a route war is going on and airlines drop fares to stay even with the competition. One of the best ways to anticipate these fare drops is to keep in touch with friends who work in the airline industry. They often hear rumblings before the fares are actually lowered. On occasion, the *Wall Street Journal* also carries news of fare breaks before they happen.

For airfares, check the Sunday travel and entertainment sections of newspapers published in gateway cities closest to where you live (ads sometimes appear in weekday editions, too). When you're about the same distance from two or more major airports, check them all out. Fares are often much cheaper on some routes than others, even though the mileage is approximately the same or varies by two or three hundred miles. For example, there have been times when the lowest round-trip fare from Dallas–Fort Worth is $153, while it's $418 from New Orleans; $309 from New York; and $175 from Washington, D.C.

Fast action is required in taking advantage of these deals, as the time period when tickets are available is short and the number of tickets is limited. However, if you don't succeed in obtaining tickets through a specific airline's offer, call competing airlines on the route who may have decided to match the advertising airline's prices but have not gone public with the information.

Don't give up if only the more expensive tickets are available for the dates you want to travel. Although the airline reservationists may have sold all the cheap tickets allotted to a particular flight, discounted tickets for that flight may be obtained from other sources. Airlines don't want to lose money, and every unsold seat on a flight represents lost income. Therefore, when they anticipate light loads on various routes, the airlines sell blocks of tickets at greatly reduced rates to wholesalers, who in turn sell their unsold inventory to discounters.

Airlines also sell these tickets directly to travel agencies that specialize in discounting. Although these so-called bucket shops used to have "here today, gone tomorrow" reputations, as years have passed most have become reliable business operations. You'll find their advertisements in the travel sections of Sunday newspapers.

Discounted tickets frequently come without some of the requirements for tickets bought from the airlines, such as advance purchase. But this is often counterbalanced by other restrictions. Discounted tickets are almost always nonendorsable, which means they can be used only on the issuing airline. This means that when a flight is cancelled, you're out of luck until there's space on one of that airline's subsequent flights. Also, most of the tickets are stamped "nonrefundable," so they cannot be returned for a refund of the list price. Before you advance any money, it's a good idea to check with the Better Business Bureau if you have any doubts regarding a discounter. If it's possible, also pay with a credit card rather than a check or money order.

Among the companies that advertise discounted tickets are Maharaja/Consumer Wholesale Travel, 34 W. 33rd Street, Suite 1014, New York, NY 10001; 212/213-2020 in New York; 800/223-6862 elsewhere in the United States; and TFI Tours International, 34 W. 37th Street, 12th floor, New York, NY 10001; 212/736-1140 in New York; 800/825-3834 elsewhere in the United States. Also, major metropolitan newspaper travel sections almost always contain the advertisements of ticket brokers in their respective areas.

In addition to the regularly scheduled commercial flights, a number of charter airlines also fly to San Francisco. The best way to find out about flights that originate in your part of the country is by contacting travel agents or keeping your ears open for any group trips that are in the offing. For example, college alumni associations, fraternal organizations, and other groups often arrange trips in which people who aren't members can participate. Since charter tour wholesalers often buy their hotel accommodations at deeply discounted rates, charter air-and-accommodations packages are often good buys. If you have contracted with a reliable organization, such as an alumni association, you should get your money back if the charter company defaults or the trip is cancelled because not enough people have signed on for it.

Sometimes, when you join a discount travel club, you can defy the rule that booking flights early saves you money. Simply put (and it's a fairly complicated subject), travel suppliers (wholesalers who buy blocks of tickets from airlines, hotels, and the like) are often left with unsold inventory. Naturally, they would like to get some money back on this part of their investment, even if it's much less than they would ordinarily receive. Discount travel clubs help the suppliers get rid of the inventory by offering complete tour and cruise packages, seats on charter flights, and occasionally seats on scheduled flights at a fraction of their regular prices—from 15 to 60 percent off, in most cases—to members on a "last-minute" basis (actually it can be a week or even a month in advance). In exchange for yearly membership fees, which generally cost from $20 to $50, members are given access to a toll-free hot-line number to call regarding "last-minute" travel bargains. Some clubs also send newsletters to their subscribers, telling them about offers that are available. Among the discount clubs currently in operation which handle San Francisco airline tickets are:

Encore/Short Notice, 4501 Forbes Blvd., Lanham, MD 20706; 301/459-8020 ($49.95, with a free thirty-day trial available).

Last-Minute Travel, 1249 Boylston Street, Boston, MA 02215; 800/LAST-MIN. (This is a travel agency with no membership fee.)

Traveler's Advantage, 3033 S. Parker Road, Suite 1000, Aurora, CO 80014; 800/548-1116 ($49 membership fee).

However you choose to fly, pay for your ticket with your charge card if by so doing your bags are automatically insured.

Other Ways of Getting There

When you're planning to travel to San Francisco by car, determine the most direct (or scenic, or historically interesting) route by phoning an auto club such as the American Automobile Association (AAA). Although having a car is convenient if you want to make any excursions out of San Francisco, parking in The City is expensive when you're staying at a downtown hotel. Motor hotels near Fisherman's Wharf and across the bay in Emeryville and Alameda are among the properties away from The City's center that have free on-site parking.

Even if you have a car, you'll probably want to plan on taking public transportation while you're in San Francisco. Driving can be difficult when you're not used to heavy traffic or hills and are unfamiliar with the territory.

San Francisco is also served by **Amtrak** (800/USA-RAIL)

from the north, south, and east. Whether or not you consider train travel a bargain will depend upon the distance you have to cover. Shuttle buses transport passengers to and from depots in Oakland and Emeryville, and the Ferry Building and CalTrain station in downtown San Francisco.

You can get to San Francisco by bus, too. The City is served by Greyhound. Buses arrive at and depart from the Transbay Terminal (425 Mission Street; 800/231-2222), only a short taxi ride from major hotels, but the bargain aspects of bus fares have to be balanced against the same factors as railroad travel. Travel by charter bus is another matter, and is covered later in the chapter under "Packaged Travel."

In the event you decide to travel by train or bus, check to see what advance purchase options are available or if any special promotions will be going on during the dates you'll be free.

Speaking of dates, when you have some flexibility with travel time, you'll most likely be able to save more than when you don't. Traveling on certain days of the week, at certain times of the year, and purchasing tickets in advance—often as much as ninety days—can greatly affect the prices you have to pay for airline tickets as well as other forms of public transportation.

Accommodations Advance Work

As a first step in choosing where to stay, write to the San Francisco Convention and Visitors Bureau for the "San Francisco Accommodations" brochure ($2, see chapter 13 for the address). You also might go to your local telephone company office or library and spend some time with a San Francisco telephone directory's display ads in the hotel and motel section of the Yellow Pages. Phone those hotels that sound appealing (and have toll-free numbers) for rates. Write to those that don't have toll-frees for rate sheets (see chapter 2, Bedtime Bargains). It's also a good idea to collect as many hotel brochures as you can. Rooms, gardens, and pool areas are photographed from their most flattering angles, so pictures aren't a completely reliable source of information. However, if the photos don't appeal to you, there's a very good chance the hotel or motel won't either.

Check metropolitan newspaper travel sections prior to your arrival for advertisements of special hotel packages and deals. And don't neglect to check out the *San Francisco Examiner* too, since ads for local lodging frequently appear in its travel section. For example, in the fall and early winter of 1997, the Airport Hilton featured a fascinating promotion. Upon checkout, room rates were matched to the lowest overnight temperature the day before. If the temperature got down to 43 degrees, the room cost $43 a night.

Time Management

When you have more than minimal time to plan, send for information about The City's attractions so you'll be able to prioritize them according to your interest in relation to their respective costs. Unfortunately, if we haven't done our vacation homework well, it's only after we arrive home that we learn about great attractions that we missed.

Valuable time and money can be saved by obtaining good maps—including those of public transportation routes—in advance of your trip. With a bit of study, you'll be able to plan your days' activities to save time which otherwise may be spent backtracking because you were unfamiliar with the lay of the land.

If there's any chance you might rent a car on your trip, another important prevacation task is to review the terms of your auto insurance regarding rental vehicles. Some credit cards automatically provide insurance if you use your card for the rental, so check to see if yours does.

For people who have disabilities or special needs that influence their travel, it's especially important to plan ahead. San Francisco is quite an accessible city, with the usual ramping, special public rest room facilities, and modified hotel rooms.

Financial Planning

To avoid posttrip trauma, sometime during the planning process you'll need to decide how much time and money you can afford to spend. Though the average visitor spends between four and five nights in San Francisco and spends $170.30 a day (convention delegates spend an average of $267.25 per day), you can have a great time for a lot less. That's because the average visitor probably doesn't know how (or care) to get the most for his or her money.

Whatever amount you budget for your trip, be realistic. If you fail to bring along sufficient money or traveler's checks to cover the cash you'll need, it will mean a lot of unnecessary expense.

While there are hundreds of ATMs in San Francisco that take Cirrus (800-4-CIRRUS), Plus (800-THE-PLUS), and other major cards, hotels in general do not cash personal checks for anyone who isn't a hotel guest. Even then, there are limits to the amount of money that will be advanced.

San Francisco banks, which are part of chains with offices in various parts of the country, will cash out-of-state checks, but usually only for people who have accounts with the system or other affiliated banks. Among them are Bank of America and Wells Fargo Bank. Two pieces of identification, such as a driver's license and bank check-cashing card or major credit card are usually necessary.

To get cash advances from charge cards is expensive. Posted rates on machines range from $5.95 to $9.95 for any amount up to $100; with $95.95 to $99.95 the tariff for obtaining $1,000.

There are check-cashing services, too, if all else fails and you're desperate, but most of them charge a whopping 20 percent on amounts up to $500, and you must have a major credit card, plus a driver's license in order to cash the check.

Packaged Travel

If independent travel is difficult or doesn't appeal to you, you'll find that many companies offer organized tours to San Francisco. Most of them, however, include other California destinations as well, such as Yosemite National Park, Lake Tahoe, the Wine Country, Monterey, and Carmel—even Los Angeles and Disneyland. The best way to find out about tours that leave from your area is by phoning a number of travel agencies.

Several of the airlines serving San Francisco also offer tours. Some, like Delta Air Lines, can provide you with brochures describing what's available, including a list of hotels and the various prices. Others, like American Airlines, ask travelers to specify the components they want and the airline then comes up with a package price.

Using Your Head

Packing your mind with information on San Francisco before you leave home will provide you with mental baggage of the positive kind, as it will save you both money and time after you've arrived on the scene. For example, you'll save dialing time when you know that the area code for San Francisco and Marin County is 415, it's 510 for Contra Costa and Alameda counties across the bay to the east. If you have problems with nature calling at inconvenient times or are traveling with children, you'll probably want to invest in the *San Francisco Potty Guide* ($8.95, Handley Brown Publishing Co., P.O. Box 640725-D, San Francisco, CA 94164).

You'll also save time, money, and frustration by obtaining a detailed map of San Francisco before you leave home. Although the San Francisco Convention and Visitors Bureau provides some good ones, you may want to augment them with a commercial map, such as Flashmaps San Francisco. The map, which sells for $8.95 and is available in bookstores, includes seating diagrams of Herbst Theater, Symphony Hall, and the War Memorial Opera House; of Candlestick Park (now called 3–Com Park) and the Oakland–Alameda County Coliseum Complex and Stadium, locations of churches, art galleries, and museums, and architectural points of interest in The City as well as wineries in the Sonoma and Napa valleys.

If your itinerary's well organized and you know exactly when you'll want to rent cars for day trips and excursions, make the arrangements before you leave home and you'll usually be money ahead. Hertz, Budget, and Avis all had recent nationwide advertising campaigns that featured $25-a-day weekend rentals and reduced weekly rates as well.

People who really plan ahead can save by obtaining a charge card that gives flight miles for every dollar charged. If you charge everything on that card—groceries, gas, clothes, dry cleaning, appliances, jewelry, cosmetics, and cleaning products—and pay the balance off every month, chances are you'll be able to get a ticket for the price of the annual fee(s) during the period it took to get sufficient points.

Problem-Proof Packing

If you haven't done your homework, it's quite possible to stuff the absolutely wrong stuff in your bags. Since San Francisco is, after all, in California, first-time visitors often assume that it's warm like Los Angeles or even Palm Springs. What they don't realize is that the state is hundreds of miles long from its Mexican to Oregon borders, and that San Francisco is north of the halfway point. Add, also, the fact that from June to August morning and evening fog pushes through the Golden Gate and swirls over the Marin County headlands. Whether or not the fog shrouds downtown, it usually begins to burn off at mid-morning, only to return in the late afternoon. As a result, summer months have their share of days when it feels colder than some weeks in winter.

Typical summer clothes which are appropriate in other parts of the country, therefore, almost never are comfortable in The City. There is the occasional warm day, of course, when the temperature soars to 80 or higher. But that doesn't happen very often. As soon as you move inland, however, summer days are usually warm.

The days in the month of February through May are generally clear and sunny, but for the very finest weather, it's September to mid-October. However, there are no hard-and-fast weather rules for the San Francisco Bay area. Winter days, traditionally the rainy season, can be incredibly fine.

Whether your trip is for business or pleasure, it should be easier to decide what to pack by consulting the chart below, which includes the average daily mean maximum and minimum temperatures in degrees Fahrenheit by month as well as average inches of rainfall.

	Daily Mean Maximum	Daily Mean Minimum	Rainfall Total Inches
January	56.1	46.2	4.48
February	59.4	48.4	2.83
March	60.0	48.6	2.58
April	61.1	49.2	1.48
May	62.5	50.7	0.35
June	64.3	52.5	0.15
July	64.0	53.1	0.04
August	65.0	54.2	0.08
September	68.9	55.8	0.24
October	68.3	54.8	1.09
November	62.9	51.5	2.49
December	56.9	47.2	3.52

Temperatures seldom rise above 70 degrees (21 degrees Celsius) or fall below 40 degrees (5 degrees Celsius).

Although dress standards have relaxed somewhat in recent years, San Franciscans dress more formally than people in most other California cities. This is especially true in the downtown district, where businesspeople dress as conservatively as anywhere in the country. Remember that you're in town to see the sights, not to be one of them. If you wear the same outfit five days in a row, it's likely no one will notice or care.

You will, however, want to pay special attention to choosing the shoes you'll bring. Since there's so much to see and do in San Francisco (and I don't want to lose a minute because of aching feet), I wear the most comfortable low-heeled shoes in my closet and bring along another equally comfortable pair. I also carry a supply of moleskin strips in my pocket to put over any tender spots *before* blisters develop.

When you travel by car, or course, you can pack the trunk solid with clothes for every clime and situation. But if you're arriving by plane, you'll save money by keeping your luggage light. Instead of taking a taxi, you can take public transportation to your hotel or motel. And if, by chance, you haven't made room reservations, you won't have to settle for less than satisfactory accommodations because the hassle of moving mountains of luggage compels you to take the first room you can get.

You may not have thought much about the economic importance of what you pack in your bag unless at some time in your travels you've had to buy toothpaste from a hotel vending machine or a pair of overpriced sunglasses from the gift shop.

There are a number of items you might pack that will save scads of money and won't weigh you down. Plastic margarine tubs, plastic glasses, plastic cutlery, and a can opener (the type you buy for picnics that can open bottles as well) will let you breakfast and lunch on cereal, berries, cottage cheese, and other items from the grocery store.

The articles in an emergency kit (a few Band-Aids, safety pins, pain reliever, needle and thread, digestive tablets, and sunblock) may not necessarily be used, but if they are, they will save you dollars, too. Put the items in a plastic storage bag with gripper closing so that you can find them easily when they're needed.

HOW TO BE COOL IN SAN FRANCISCO

If you hate to have that "obvious tourist" feeling, the following dos and don'ts will make you blend right in with the San Francisco crowd.

1. Never wear white shoes—except running shoes when you're jogging.

2. Never refer to The City as Frisco.

3. Don't request "I Left My Heart in San Francisco" at the piano bar.

4. Don't stare at couples—whether they're male and female or same sex—holding hands, walking with their arms around each other, or kissing. San Francisco has the largest per capita gay population of any North American city, and an air of openness prevails.

5. Save your shorts for the beach and excursions outside The City. They're not appropriate in-town apparel except for jogging.

When you forget any health or beauty aids and are staying at a downtown hotel, it will pay to go to a drugstore or Woolworths (by the cable car turnaround at the corner of Market and Powell) rather than patronizing the vending machines found in many hotels or motels. Upscale hotels generally will provide you with complimentary toothbrushes, razors, and the like if you request them.

Don't forget to bring your umbrella, regardless of the season. An extra copy of your eyeglasses prescription, tucked in your wallet, may come in handy, too. And since San Francisco is a great shopping city, you'll want to pack a lightweight carry-on bag in your luggage so that you'll have a means of transporting your purchases home.

CHAPTER

2

Bedtime Bargains

San Francisco hotel rooms have the reputation of being among the most expensive in the United States, and that may be true if you're comparing rack (published) rates. But San Francisco, with more than 30,500 hotel rooms, is also known as a place where you can get good deals on accommodations if you know how to find them.

The published rates of The City's luxury hotels go from about $200 to $400 a night. Expect a minimum rack rate of at least $100 to $160 if you're interested in attractive lodgings in a good location. According to a *Wall Street Journal* survey of hotel rates in December 1996, foreign travel and heavily discounted airline fares had resulted in 90 percent room occupancy in some months, and average San Francisco room rates as high as $150 a night.

Most of San Francisco's hotels were purpose-built, but a few of them have been converted from other uses. For example, the swanky Ritz Carlton on Nob Hill occupies an imposing building that used to be the West Coast headquarters of the Metropolitan Life Insurance Company. Many of the hotels are spruced-up reincarnations of the residence hotels of yesteryear. Down-at-the-heels hotels—respectable in their day— have been perked up with paint and decorator fabrics. The interiors of former fleabags have been completely gutted and transformed into chic and functional hotels. The result is an unusually large number of smaller "boutique" hotels. As you might imagine, conversions have succeeded to varying degrees (I'll never forget a chilly night spent in a drafty but otherwise charming conversion with radiators hissing and clanging until it was time to get up).

Be cautious about reserving rooms in hotels whose rack rates are in the $45 to $79 range until you have seen them. Chances are that although the hotel may be acceptable, it will be in an undesirable area. One historic hotel that has recently been restored is located next to a housing project. Also, be wary when a hotel advertises that it is directly on the cable car line. The location may sound convenient, but rooms facing the street can be very noisy.

Views from most street-side hotel rooms in San Francisco are fascinating, and from the upper floors can be downright colossal. However, downtown San Francisco seems to be one of the noisier cities in the country no matter the hour—cars and buses braking on the hills, the wail of police sirens floating from the elevated freeways, cable cars rattling down the tracks. Therefore, if you're a light sleeper, you may be happier forgoing the view and requesting an inside room.

Finding the Bargains

I am continually amazed to find that there are people who pay the first rate they're quoted by a hotel, without even asking if any discounts or package deals are available. By being aware of the kinds of bargains that are possible, you'll save hundreds of dollars on accommodations—the biggest single expense on most vacations.

The quality of the accommodations you get for your money depends a lot upon the effort you spend in researching various alternatives. People whose travel dates are flexible usually get the lowest rates, but there are bargains to be had even during the busiest times of the year. However, it's a rare reservationist who volunteers the information that there are deals available. You have to ask for them.

Air-and-accommodations packages are sometimes the most

economical ways to procure San Francisco lodgings. However, you can't take it for granted that they will be your best deal. In 1997 you could get an air-and-three-night accommodations package, Kansas City–San Francisco, from American Airlines Flyaway Vacations (800/321-2121) for $978. As with most airline packages, the airfare was supposedly based on the lowest current rate, which was $269. Accommodations were at the **Handlery Union Square Hotel** (351 Geary Street; 415/781-7800), one of my favorite places to stay in San Francisco because of its pleasant rooms, convenient location, and outdoor heated pool. The package price also included departure taxes and transfers to and from San Francisco International Airport.

At the time that particular package was available, the lowest available airfare offered to the general public was $118 round-trip, and flying on Tuesday, Wednesday, or Saturday, with a fourteen-day advance purchase. The going rate at the Handlery was $145 per night for a double room. As late as April, some dates were also available for the hotel's "Honeymoon Package," which included a bottle of champagne, a box of chocolates, a gardenia, and two one-day cable car passes for $134 for the first night and $109 for subsequent nights. Although at some times the air-and-accommodations package might have been a bargain, its price was definitely beaten by travelers who took the time to investigate all of their options.

Throughout 1997, Delta Dream Vacations offered a two-night package with a choice of hotels, one of which was the Handlery. The package, which included airport transfers and two-for-one rates for five different tours, cost $569 per person from New York and $469 from Dallas–Fort Worth (packages were not available from Kansas City). These prices represented good deals if you couldn't get round-trip tickets for less than $400 from New York or $300 from Dallas–Fort Worth.

When you inquire about promotions, it may pay dividends to tell the reservationist where you live. In 1997, for example, the Handlery had a "Kamaaina Rate" for residents of

Hawaii—$115 a night for standard and superior rooms and $135 for club rooms (larger rooms with amenities such as balconies, hair dryers, robes, and nightly turndown service).

You'll find promotional ads for individual properties in metropolitan newspaper travel sections as well as in travel magazines. Most of these offer the rooms at bargain prices and are calculated to keep occupancy rates up during periods when they tend to dip. Since they're good deals, you have to act quickly, as rooms at the advertised price are subject to availability.

One of the hotels that frequently advertises in newspapers is the **Maxwell** (formerly the Rafael). From the moment you step into the lobby (386 Geary Street; 415/986-2000), you feel like you're in Europe. The lobby and guest rooms exude charm. Rack rates are listed at $115 to $135; the 1997 "Choose Your View" package included free parking (usual charge, $17), continental breakfast, and two tickets to either the SkyDeck at Embarcadero Center, "UnderWater World" at Pier 39, or a Blue and Gold bay cruise. The package costs $135 for a standard and $155 for a deluxe room.

Hotels that cater to conventions and business travelers often lower their prices on weekends. These sweet deals frequently are unadvertised, and tourists who don't ask about specials will find themselves paying top prices. Many hotels are reluctant to publish their rack rates, since the prices they charge are demand-driven. As the sales manager at a major San Francisco hotel says, "We're a convention hotel, so during periods when we have a lot of convention business, our rates are maybe one hundred dollars higher than they are on the following weekend."

While people generally are aware of the fact that you can buy airline tickets at a discount, many of them don't know that you can get hotel rooms at greatly reduced rates by joining a club or merely by calling a hotel discount hot line.

According to *Consumer Reports Travel Letter*, Entertainment Publications' "Ultimate Travel Directory" (800/445-4137) contains "by far the largest number of hotels available through any single half-price listing (3,737 hotels in the United States)."

These half-price listings give you 50 percent off the hotel's rack rate, which may be higher than the "selling" rate. Therefore, that 50 percent off may not be a true half-price. However, there are times when you can't find a better deal. The 50 percent discounts are limited by availability, which means the dates when those who decide these things don't expect their hotels to be more than 80 percent full. The directory costs $59.95.

Traveler's Advantage, affiliated with Entertainment Publications, Inc., is a discount travel club that recruits members in a number of ways. For example, department stores and supermarkets occasionally advertise three-month trial memberships in Traveler's Advantage for $1, which includes a certificate for one night's free hotel stay at Choice Hotels, Travelodge, La Quinta, Days Inn, Howard Johnson, Ramada, Rodeway, EconoLodge, or MainStay Suites. Travelodge San Francisco Center (1707 Market Street; 415/621-6775), Clarion Bedford Hotel at Union Square (761 Post Street; 415/673-6040 or 800/227-5642), and Comfort Inn by the Bay (2775 Van Ness Avenue; 415/928-5000 or 800/221-2222) are the participating San Francisco properties.

In addition, members get a "Hotels at Half Price" directory, which lists more than three dozen San Francisco hotels, including several that are among The City's best. Yearly membership in Traveler's Advantage is $49.

These memberships don't always work to your advantage, however. Though I have known people who have been able to reserve rooms at low rates, my efforts have only occasionally paid off. For example, all of the San Francisco Choice Hotels in the free room/night program (with the exception of the Airport Comfort Inn in South San Francisco) were blacked out for April 1997, and no rooms were available at the Travelodge for the same period. Availability of half-price hotels was a mixed bag. While several hotels had rooms available, the savings on the going rate was usually only a few dollars. Reservationists say that during periods when there are no big conventions in town and the weather is drizzly, deeper discounts are obtainable.

Central Reservation Services advertises a free hot line (800/548-3311) for last-minute discounts on hotels in San Francisco, including the Best Western Flamingo (114 7th Street; 415/621-0701 or 800/444-5818), Best Western Americana (121 7th Street; 415/626-0200 or 800/444-5816), Best Western Carriage Inn (140 7th Street; 415/552-8600 or 800/444-5817, Renoir (45 McAllister Street; 415/626-5200 or 800/576-3388), Savoy (580 Geary Street; 415/441-2700 or 800/227-4223, and Holiday Inn at Fisherman's Wharf (1300 Columbus Avenue; 415/771-9000 or 800/HOLIDAY).

Hotel Reservations Network (800/96-HOTEL) advertises savings of up to 65 percent off the rack rates of several San Francisco properties. Both of these services are free. Whether you're successful in getting the accommodations you want is largely a matter of luck. If the hotel has last-minute cancellations or lower occupancy than anticipated, you'll get your rooms at bargain prices.

Among the best hotel values in The City are those of the Kimpton Group. These fourteen "boutique" hotels are properties which, after their purchase by the organization, were completely renovated and refurbished. They are well-located, attractive hotels, most of which feature guest rooms in the $100 to $200 range. However, frequent promotions at all of the hotels either lower the rates or add value to them by including important freebies.

One of the Kimpton Group hotels with the least expensive rooms, **Monticello Inn** (127 Ellis Street; 415/392-8800 or 800/669-7777; rack rate, $109) was built in 1906 and is located just a block from the Powell Street cable car line. In 1996 a special cut the room rate to $89, which included complimentary continental breakfast and afternoon wine. Monticello parking costs are an additional $16 a day.

Another Kimpton Group hotel is the **Juliana,** one of the first to be acquired. Located at the corner of Bush and Stockton streets (590 Bush Street; 415/392-2540 or 800/328-3880 outside California), it's only a block from China-town's main artery, Grant Avenue, and two blocks through the Stockton Tunnel from Union Square. Appointed with floral fabrics and traditional furniture, the Juliana's atmosphere makes you feel like you're staying in the guest room of a friend's home. Rack rate for single or double rooms are priced from $129 to $179 a night, and junior suites, $169 and $189. Rates include complimentary morning limousine service to the Financial District, morning coffee, and evening wine. Parking fees are not included.

During December 1996, the Juliana offered a "Save Like the Dickens" package for $169, which included a suite and two tickets to see Dickens's *A Christmas Carol,* presented by the American Conservatory Theater (ACT).

During the holiday season, hotels all over San Francisco offer special holiday packages, some at half their regular rates. In 1996, the Galleria Park hotel's (191 Sutter Street; 415/781-3060 or 800/792-9639) "Mistletoe Madness" package ($79) included deluxe accommodations for two, morning coffee, evening wine, and fitness room privileges. For $109, complimentary parking and continental breakfast were added. Usual rack rate at the Galleria Park is from $170 to 190 for a double.

The **Mandarin Oriental's** (222 Sansome Street; 415/885-0999) "Shop, Skate, and Slumber package, at $259, consisted of a deluxe room, two passes for ice rink skating, complimentary parking, and a complimentary dessert for package participants who dined at the hotel's restaurant. The usual rate for deluxe rooms is $350.

Hotel Nikko's (222 Mason Street; 415/394-1111) holiday package, at $139, included a deluxe room ($179 for a room on the concierge floor), valet parking, free gift wrapping, plus use of the fitness center, sauna, and glass-enclosed pool. The rack rates are $245 (one person), $275 (two people) for the deluxe rooms and $285 or $315 for those on the concierge floor.

Rooms at the **Clift Hotel** (495 Geary Street; 415/775-4700) are usually pricier than most of us want to pay, with double-room rates from $225 to $370 (weekends, $195 to $265). With the 1996 "Wrap It Up in Style" holiday package, rooms went for as little as $150 per night, and as part of the bargain, guests could have up to ten packages elegantly gift wrapped each day of their stay.

In hotel room pricing, it's a given that the higher the rate, the more deeply it's apt to be discounted, especially during slow periods of the year. After all, the bottom line looks far worse when one hundred $265 rooms are vacant than when their rate is $105. To get those big-money rooms filled, management has to make them competitive with rooms in less luxurious hotels. As a result, you can often get the most bang for your accommodations buck by seeking out the upper-tier hotels that offer promotions you can't afford to ignore. At times, the room price isn't cut dramatically, but amenities are added to make guests feel pampered.

For example, the **Huntington Hotel** on Nob Hill (415/474-5400) "1997 Romance Package," priced at $215 per couple per night, included a luxury room overlooking Huntington Park or The City, a chilled bottle of champagne, and formal tea or sherry service upon arrival plus use of the hotel's chauffeured sedan for nearby business meetings or shopping at Union Square. Rack rate at the Huntington for a luxury room is about $250.

The **Grand Hyatt San Francisco**'s "Heart of the City Romance Package" (345 Stockton Street; 415/398-1234), offered throughout 1997, included a deluxe room for two with a walkout balcony and views of The City or the bay, a bottle of Domaine Chandon champagne, and a souvenir book, *The Best Places to Kiss in Northern California*. Also included were complimentary valet parking (hotel parking rates are $24 a day) and breakfast for two in the Plaza Restaurant or breakfast in bed. The package, based on space availability, cost $249 per room per night. Regular rack rate for the same category of accommodations is $275. Weekend rates, also subject to availability, are only $184. Obviously, if you plan to stay at the Hyatt, the package saves money on weekdays and provides a couple of fancy extras. However, if you are in San Francisco on a weekend, haven't arrived by car, don't drink, and have no interest in kissing spots, you'll save by using the weekend rate and buying your own breakfast.

Like most San Francisco hotels, the Grand Hyatt offers its best deals between November 1 and the first part of January (excluding New Year's Eve). The 1996 "Holiday Shopping Package" included complimentary valet parking, discounted theater tickets, plus savings and special events at Macy's ($169). From December 15 to January 6 (excluding December 31), the hotel also offered a "Savvy Shoppers Rate" of $119 for a double room.

Unless business reasons or specific sight-seeing objectives compel you to stay in a certain hotel, you'll do better financially if you investigate all of your lodging options. You'll find that most motels are away from the center of town and that many of them provide free parking. However, even motel room prices are higher in San Francisco than in comparable motels in less populated parts of the country.

For example, **Super 8 Motel** (2440 Lombard Street; 415/992-0244) has a published rate of $70 to $99 for a double. However, in spring 1997 actual rates were $69.88 for a one-bed room and $74.88 for two beds—and those prices were before discounts such as the 10 percent from AAA or the American Association of Retired Persons (AARP) were applied. Parking is free and a Muni (short for Municipal Railway) bus stop is close by. As a rule, the farther away from the city center motels are located, the better chance they'll be in an acceptable neighborhood.

A SUITE SPLURGE

When your idea of heaven is a room with an incredible view and you can squeeze an extra few hundred dollars out of your travel budget, spend a couple of days during your San Francisco stay in a suite on one of the hotel's top floors.

After you've stayed in a hotel for a night or two, go down to the reception desk and ask how much it would cost to upgrade to a suite. If a good percentage of the property's suites are unoccupied, you may find it costs far less than you would imagine. In fact, you might even have a choice of suites, so check out the views before you decide. Also, by choosing the night(s) you splurge, you can better determine if the weather will be ideal for maximizing those views.

Of all the San Francisco hotel suites with unbeatable views I've stayed in, my vote goes to the Bayview Suite on the thirty-first floor of Park Lane's **Parc Fifty-Five** (55 Cyril Magnin; 415/392-8000 or 800/227-6963). Elegantly appointed, the suite is huge and has multiple windows so that you get to look out on a good part of The City—from the South Bay to Twin Peaks. And if you want to look at San Francisco from another perspective, simply go to the Executive Lounge down the hall. Rack rate for the suite with one bedroom is $600.

In general, lodging is also less expensive in nearby towns and cities which are easily accessible by public transportation. Though you may save a good deal of money by staying in these outlying areas, you must balance your monetary savings against the time it will take you to commute. For example, the **Concord Hilton** (1970 Diamond Boulevard; 510/827-2000) has a weekend special of $89 a night, including continental breakfast. However, it's a forty-five-minute, $3.05 ride from the Concord Bay Area Rapid Transit (BART) station to the heart of downtown San Francisco.

Closer in, the **Holiday Inn–Bay Bridge** in Emeryville (off

Interstate Highway 80 via the Powell-Emeryville exit; 510/547-7888) costs $95 for a double both on weeknights and weekends and is a twenty- to twenty-five-minute, $2 ride away from The City by BART. Rooms with spectacular views of the bay and San Francisco are available at the same price, but for them you must make reservations at least a week in advance. Visitors combining business with pleasure in the Bay Area may want to stay at one of the hotels near the airport. They are generally a bit less expensive than comparable rooms in the heart of The City.

If your budget allows you to spend no more than $30 or $40 per person for lodging each night, head for the visitor center at Hallidie Plaza to check out the racks for discount and special deal coupons. There are always several available for lower-price hotels. While you're there, look for the "Traveler Discount Lodging Guide," which is full of accommodations coupons, among them several for San Francisco, including four Holiday Inns.

Correspondence Course

One of the most effective ways of finding bargains is to choose a number of hotels (from brochures, guidebooks, or tips from friends) and write directly to them requesting information about any discounts or promotions that will be in effect during your San Francisco stay. Among the hotels you might write to are:

Kensington Park (450 Post Street; 415/788-6400. Double rates start at about $115). Included in the price are complimentary breakfast, afternoon tea, and sherry. There's a small theater on the second floor of the Kensington, which makes the hotel ideal for people who want to be entertained but don't want to leave their hotel at night (the theater is dark for short periods between plays). The Kensington Park is a hotel that advertises special rates—sometimes as low as $89—in newspaper travel sections.

The **Inn at Union Square** (440 Post Street; 415/397-3510 or

800/AT-THE-INN) is an attractively decorated hotel only a half block west of Union Square. Rack rates for guest rooms are $120 to $180 and include complimentary continental breakfast, afternoon tea service, and wine with hors d'oeuvres.

Galleria Park (101 Sutter Street; 415/781-3060), whose holiday package was mentioned above, is also a good fair-weather choice, as it has a rooftop jogging track and park in addition to its fitness room. Rack rates run $170 to $190 a night, single or double.

Radisson Miyako Hotel San Francisco (1625 Post Street; 415/922-3200) in Japantown offers guest rooms in both Western and Japanese styles ($159 to $179). There are also authentic Japanese suites and a few Western-style suites with sauna. The sixteen-story hotel features a Japanese garden courtyard and shopping at Japan Center.

Alternative Arrangements

The **Marines Memorial Club** (609 Sutter Street; 415/673-6672 or 800/562-7463) gets high marks from people who have stayed there. With all the amenities of a hotel, including concierge and room service, the club also has a pool, exercise room, saunas, a theater, library, and laundry facilities. There are kitchenettes and/or fireplaces in some of the rooms, too. Rates are $70 to $110 for a double room. Originally established for the military and their families, just about everyone can stay at Marines Memorial now. There is, however, a sliding scale for room rates. The same room goes from $70 to $120 for a double, depending upon whether one is active in the military, a reservist, a veteran, a state or federal employee, with a corporation, or the guest of a member.

The better bed and breakfast establishments in good neighborhoods may cost you as much as first-class hotels, but can be a bargain for travelers who treasure a quiet night's sleep and personalized attention. The best recommendations are those of friends and business associates whose judgment you trust.

SAVINGS WITH CHARM

A rather unusual bargain—one with great dollops of charm thrown in—is the ongoing promotion offered by the Four Sisters Inns. Stay a total of six nights at three or more of the inns during a two-week period and you get the seventh night free. Stay three nights and you get the fourth night at half-price.

Since there are two inns in downtown San Francisco (**White Swan Inn** at 845 Bush Street; 415/775-1755 or 800/999-9570; and **Petit Auberge,** 863 Bush Street; 415/928-6000 or 800/365-3004), one in the Napa Valley (**Maison Fleurie,** 6529 Yount Street, Yountville; 707/944-2056 or 800/788-0369), and three in the Monterey-Carmel area (**Gosby House Inn,** 643 Lighthouse Avenue, Pacific Grove; 408/375-1287 or 800/527-8828; **Green Gables Inn,** 104 5th Street, Pacific Grove; 408/375-2095 or 800/722-1774; and **Cobblestone Inn** at Junipero between 7th and 8th Streets in Carmel; 408/625-5222 or 800/833-8836, the plan is ideal for travelers who combine their San Francisco visit with excursions to the Wine Country or Carmel.

All of the inn's rates include large country breakfasts—often eggs, sausages, crepes, fruit, and more—always hearty enough to keep you going until dinner time. Other perks include morning newspapers, complimentary beverages, afternoon tea, home-baked cookies to snack on, valet parking in San Francisco, and complimentary use of bicycles in the other locations.

Nightly room rates range from $90 to $220 for a double, the price depending on the inn's location and the type of accommodation selected. Most rooms cost $160 a night or less. Even if you average $160 a night for six nights, the average drops to $137 when you divide the total cost for six nights by seven.

One of the most unusual B and Bs is the **Red Victorian** (1665 Haight Street; 415/864-1978) in the Haight-Ashbury. Built in 1904 as a country resort hotel, its eighteen upstairs guest rooms commemorate the Summer of Love (one of the bathrooms, which are shared, is named the Love Bathroom). Amenities include a meditation room and motivational videotapes. Rates range from $86 to $126 a night ($26 to $35 lower per night for stays of seven to fourteen days).

When you plan to be in San Francisco for an extended period of time—or even a week or two—you might want to consider renting an apartment. While per night rates are often comparable to what you would pay for a hotel room, you usually get more space for your money. Then, too, the savings on dining can be significant when you can prepare some of your own meals.

Executive Suites (415/495-5151) offers apartments with maid service, modern kitchens, cookware, tableware, linens, complimentary newspapers, free local phone service, and free use of fitness centers, a swimming pool, jacuzzi, and sauna at most locations. Parking is available on or adjacent to all locations for an additional fee. Weekly rates go from $159 to $199 a night for up to thirteen nights; $139 to $159 per night for two weeks to twenty-nine nights, and $95 to $105 per night for thirty nights or more. Parking is not included.

Three facilities affiliated with **Hostelling International** (HI) are located in San Francisco and its environs. HI–San Francisco Downtown (312 Mason Street; 415/788-5604) and HI–San Francisco Fisherman's Wharf provide inexpensive lodging in convenient city locations. The downtown hostel features semiprivate rooms with 24-hour access, free nightly movies, walking tours, and special events. Rates are $14 to $16 for HI members.

For the same price (half price for those under 18 when with a parent), the Fisherman's Wharf hostel (Building 240, Fort Mason; 415/771/7277) is located in a scenic wooded area overlooking San Francisco Bay and the Golden Gate Bridge. Muni no. 42 buses stop at Northpoint and Van Ness Avenue, an easy walking distance away.

The third hostel occupies two historic 1907 buildings five miles north of the Golden Gate Bridge in Sausalito (Building 941, Fort Barry; 415/331-2777). Near beaches, rolling hills, and hiking trails, the Marin Headlands hostel has both dormitory-style bedrooms and family rooms at $12 to $14 a night, per person.

Sleep well.

CHAPTER

3

Solving the Dining Dilemma

San Francisco ranks as the restaurant capital of the United States, with more eating places per thousand residents than any other metropolitan area. That statistic in itself doesn't mean much. What's important is that San Francisco restaurants also get very high marks as far as food and ambience are concerned.

While some of these elite eateries are presided over by name chefs who prepare dinners that cost $75 and more (without wine), you can dine at most restaurants for far less. In fact, it's fairly easy to find places with lots of atmosphere where two people can eat very well and spend less than $30 for dinner. And less than $20 at some.

Obviously, reviewing even 5 percent of The City's restaurants—there are an estimated 3,300 of them—is beyond the scope of this book. What follows is merely a small sampling. We have divided them into traditional, ethnic, trendy, delicatessen, and miscellaneous categories. Since seafood is an integral part of most restaurants' culinary repertoires, we haven't categorized it separately. And we have not included hash houses or lunch counters, simply because there isn't enough space.

Most of the restaurants that have opened in the past couple

of years have been in the South of Market Street area (SoMa)—currently the hottest place to dine. Out of the twenty-three restaurants that began business in 1996, nine were in the SoMa area. The traditionals are mainly downtown, though a few of them are in the neighborhoods.

Starting Out the Day Right

One of the easiest ways to cut food costs is by eating breakfast at restaurants, or at coffee and muffin/bagel/pastry stands, rather than at your hotel. Spend some time on the first morning of your stay walking about and looking for no-nonsense cafes, such as **Sears Fine Foods Restaurant** at 439 Powell Street (415/986-1160; try the Swedish pancakes), which look clean and bustle with business and other places that sell breakfast foods from their counters. Since San Francisco is a commuter town where lots of businesspeople and office workers have breakfast after they get to The City, you'll find many eateries downtown that cater to a regular breakfast trade.

When you don't need a big ham-and-eggs, fill 'er up breakfast, walk along Grant Avenue until you find a Chinese bakery with a few tables and booths. Point at the items in the glass case that you would like to try. You may have some gastronomic surprises, but it's lots of fun. To be on the safe side, order a pork-filled bun and an almond cookie—not your regular breakfast, but after all, you *are* on vacation.

Follow Grant Avenue or Stockton Street—it parallels Grant Avenue—to North Beach for an Italian breakfast. Maybe capuccino and biscotti at one of the bakeries or cafes. (At the Italian **French Baking Company of San Francisco**; 1501 Grant Avenue; 415/421-3796; you can get homemade biscotti in a variety of flavors for $5.65 a pound.) Or perhaps you might prefer foccacia and ripe *teleme* cheese at **Liguria Bakery** (1700 Stockton Street; 415/421-3786). Again, not a traditional breakfast, but San Francisco isn't a very traditional place.

Almost every savvy traveler I know does a certain amount of in-room eating—and I don't mean by ordering from room service. Snacks, fresh fruit, pastries, beverages, yogurt, cheese and crackers (keep perishables in the ice bucket) will shave dollars off the amounts you spend on regular meals. Above all, avoid using anything—no matter how tempting— in the mini-bar of your hotel room. Most mini-bar items cost four times or more than if you bought them at a market.

Supermarket Sweep

As far as markets are concerned, the small corner stores are where many San Franciscans do their grocery shopping. Therefore, those in the heart of downtown may be more expensive than those located in neighborhoods that are a mix of businesses and apartment houses. **Safeway** is the biggest supermarket chain in The City, with stores that are convenient for most tourists at 15 Marina Boulevard (415/775-4991) and 2020 Market Street (415/861-7660).

United Nations Plaza Farmers Market, at the Civic Center (Wednesday to Sunday, 7 A.M. to 5 P.M.), is a good place to get fresh fruit and vegetables, like carrots that you can eat uncooked, at reasonable prices. On the waterfront at the Ferry Building there is also the **Ferry Plaza Farmers Market** (Saturday, 8 A.M. to 1:30 P.M.), and another market at Embarcadero Center (Tuesday, 11:30 A.M. to 3 P.M.) near the Hyatt Regency. The Saturday market features special events, such as cooking classes and children's activities.

The original store of one of the best bakeries in town, **Eppler's** (750 Market Street; 415/752-0825; branches in other parts of San Francisco) is close to many of the downtown hotels. Their cheesecake has been a San Francisco favorite since the 1940s. Other popular bakeries are Specialty's Cafe and Bakery (150 Spear Street; 415/512-9550), Grain D'Or (four locations, including 665 Market Street; 415/512/8160), and Boudin Sourdough Bakery and Cafe (about a dozen locations, including several in the downtown area). And if you're any-where near the Black Muslim Bakery (160 Eddy Street; 415/929-7082), stop in for a wedge of terrific banana squash pie.

Among the best Chinatown bakeries are New Ping Yuen (1125 Stockton Street; 415/433-5571), Feng Huang Pastry (761 Jackson Street; 415/421-7885), and Golden Gate Bakery (1029 Grant Avenue; 415/781-2627).

For homemade piroshki and the like, go to the Odessa Russian Delicatessen and European Gourmet Deli (5427 Geary Boulevard; 415/666-3354 or Tip-Toe Inn Delicatessen (5423 Geary Boulevard; 415/221/6422).

People who love sourdough bread will be tempted to eat so much of it they won't have room for anything else. If you're one of them, you might consider ordering a side salad or soup in lieu of an entrée at dinner. This doesn't go over too well in expensive restaurants, but it's perfectly acceptable in the less uppity places.

When it comes to serious dining as opposed to pickup meals, emphasis should be on eating in restaurants that are typical of the area, and in San Francisco these run the gastronomic gamut from traditional, white-linen tablecloths and turn-of-the-century paneled walls to warehouse- and industrial-style eateries where pipes, ducts, supporting pil-lars, and just about every other construction element short of scaffolding become the decor. In the traditional restaurants, waiters almost always wear tuxedos, and most of them are extremely adept older men who have been waiters all their working lives. The dishes served are classics, composed of fresh ingredients, simply but impeccably prepared.

The trendy restaurants serve all sorts of food—steak in one, fusion food in another. They're not always the current rage because of a particular kind of food, but because they're perceived as *the* places to be. However, because of a celebrity chef or a new way of preparing a dish, food is very important at many of the trendies. (Remember, Bay Area chefs played an important part in developing what became known as California cuisine).

Ethnic restaurants usually attempt to either replicate their antecedents in the old country or to look as their owners think Americans of other races expect them to look. Some of the better known ethnic restaurants are gussied up while many of the storefront ethnics pay little attention to decor. As a rule, the less pretentious the place and the more it's patronized by members of the particular ethnic group, the more authentic the food. Delicatessens generally fall into ethnic categories, but since that's not always the case, we have treated them separately.

The Traditionals

Whenever we go to **John's Grill** (63 Ellis Street; 415/986-0069), I order the salmon and my longtime dining companion has the filet of sole meunière ($12.95 to $14.95), but diners eating the other fish dishes as well as the veal and beef entrées ($14.95 to $24.95) look content, too. Sam Spade's favorite, as *The Maltese Falcon* fans know, was the house specialty, rack of lamb served with baked potato and sliced tomatoes. That's what Sam's creator, Dashiell Hammett, who lived ten blocks from John's Grill, ordered too ($14.95).

John's has been around since 1908. Most of the customers are locals who have been patronizing the restaurant for years. The wood-paneled walls are lined with photos of San Francisco notables and national celebrities who have dined there. With crisp white table linen, bentwood chairs, and wall sconces, the grill is genuine San Francisco traditional. Entrées come with potatoes or rice and fresh vegetables, and portions are large.

Another one of the traditionals, **Sam's Grill** (374 Bush Street; 415/421-0594), opened in 1867 and is one of The City's best values. The classics that appeared on the menu forty years ago are still served. Clam chowder makes a delicious starter, and the French Pancakes provide a perfect ending for whatever you eat in between. The sweetbreads, broiled with bacon, are divine. But then so are the veal chops, the rex sole, and just about everything else on the menu (main courses start at about $9 and go to $21). The dark wainscoting on the walls is studded with brass coat hooks, and the curtained booths in the back room, away from the noisy front bar's hubbub, are preferred seating except for a number of regulars who stand at the bar all through lunch hour.

Though it has only been around for a couple of decades, the **Hayes Street Grill** (20 Hayes Street; 415/863-5545) is definitely a traditional seafood restaurant, with Hawaiian swordfish, ono, and yellowfin among the dozen or so kinds of fresh fish on the menu. In a mix-and-match arrangement, diners select the type of fish they want, then choose a sauce to go with it—Szechuan peanut, herbed butter with shallots, beurre blanc, and several others. There are fancier dishes, too, such as scallops with shitake and chanterelle mushrooms. If you want dessert, choose crème brulée. Entrées, which are generally served with french fries, range from $11.50 to $17.25.

Tadich Grill (240 California Street; 415/391-1849) has been in continuous operation longer than any other restaurant in California. Established as a coffee stand in 1849, it evolved into a classic fish house with legendary clam chowder, seafood salads, and such specialties as baked avocado and shrimp diablo, and petrale sole with butter sauce. Main courses cost $12 to $18. (Be sure to try the potato-based tartar sauce, whatever you order.) The wood-paneled interior, with its original mahogany bar, is classic too, with seven enclosed private booths augmenting the tables and chairs.

Tommy's Joynt (1101 Geary Boulevard; 415/775-4216) isn't at all the same sort of place as the preceding restaurants, but it's a San Francisco standard nonetheless. Food runs to thick sandwiches (Polish sausage and sauerkraut, $3.85) and hearty dishes like lamb shanks, spareribs, and beef with mashed potatoes and vegetables (dinners cost about $6 tops). The atmosphere is noisy, sometimes raucous, and the decor gets more cluttered with each passing year. Every square inch of wall space is covered with posters, advertisements, beer signs, and nostalgia plus enough junk to supply the biggest yard sale in town.

Fisherman's Wharf restaurants almost all fall into the traditional category, since their decor has been more or less standardized for at least half a century and their menus have remained virtually unchanged.

I have never had a meal to rave about at Fisherman's Wharf, but I have had memorable ones—solely because it has been such a delight looking out on the water. If you can get a window table, fine. If not, you'll probably be just as happy— and save quite a few bucks—buying a cracked crab and a loaf of French bread to eat at Aquatic Park or Marina Green (bring plenty of Handi Wipes and napkins, because it's messy).

If you have a car, want a really good seafood dinner, and are willing to forgo the view, go across the bay to **Spenger's Fish Grotto** (1919 4th Street; 510/845-7771) just off I-80 in Berkeley. It's noisy, crowded, and has served the best seafood around at reasonable prices for decades. When in doubt as to what to order, go with the fish and chips ($11.75) or shrimp scatter ($10.75). They come with great cole slaw and plates of what may be the best sourdough bread anywhere, which is replenished as a matter of course. Have a late lunch or early dinner when the place isn't so jam-packed.

Two San Francisco restaurants—though they're primarily Italian—fall into the traditional category because they've become institutions. They are **Original Joe's,** at 144 Taylor Street (415/775-4877), where the hamburgers on French rolls are terrific and the waiters wear the same style tuxes they've worn for fifty years, and **New Joe's** (347 Geary; 415/397-9999) that's patronized by people who began the ritual when they were children (ask for Joe's Special, a combination of ground beef, mushrooms, onion, garlic, and egg cooked in olive oil).

Eating Ethnic

Tibetan isn't exactly your garden-variety cuisine in North America—although it often contains vegetables—so if you would like to taste *momo* (savory stuffed dumplings), lamb simmered in vegetable broth with daikon and spinach, *churul* (blue cheese soup with minced beef), and butter tea (tea to which salt and butter have been added), go to **Lhasa Moon** (2420 Lombard Street; 415/674-9898). With white walls and hunter green trim, the decor consists of framed pictures of pre-Communist Tibet. The background music is Tibetan, too. Service is slow, but the food is surprisingly pleasing and a definite change of taste. Most meals cost less than $10 per person.

Thep-Phanom (400 Waller Street; 415/431-2526) with its folk-art decor, presents some of the best Thai food in The City. Among the standout dishes are chicken wings stuffed with glass noodles and Thai crepes. The seafood curry and beef salad are delicious, too. Entrée prices range from $5.95 to $10.95.

Le Charm (315 5th Street; 415/546-6128) is very French and very charming, with pale yellow walls and a copper-topped bar separating the kitchen and small dining room. There's also an outdoor patio where meals are served on fine days. Among the restaurant's specialties are chicken liver salad, duck confit, and salmon on a bed of spinach. Among the desserts are an orange crème brulée and French apple tart. Instead of ordering à la carte, you may choose the three-course fixed-price dinner, which costs $18. In addition to its warm atmosphere and delicious food, Le Charm boasts another plus: On-street parking is relatively easy, and there's a parking garage nearby as well.

Although its white stucco walls and French country tables

CHINESE DIM SUM AND
VIETNAMESE SANDWICHES

For inexpensive meals while expanding your gastronomic horizons, try dim sum and sandwiches made Vietnamese style. Food combinations and textures may be somewhat different than those to which you're accustomed, but to most diners, pleasingly so.

Dim sum are tidbits such as dumplings, turnovers, and steamed buns with various fillings of the kind that originally were served at Chinese teahouses. Many of us became acquainted with them at dim sum restaurants in Hong Kong. Now they've crossed the Pacific, along with the new wave of Chinese immigrants from the former Crown Colony, and have become very much the rage in San Francisco.

Every aficionado has opinions as to where you can get the best. Among the favorites is **Yank Sing Restaurant** (427 Battery Street; 415/362-1640), which offers some eighty items on the dim sum carts each day, such as snow-pea-leaf dumplings, curry chicken turnovers, tea-smoked duck, and silver-wrapped chicken ($2 to $5 per item). Others are the **Royal Jade** (675 Jackson Street; 415/392-2929), **J and J Restaurant** (615 Jackson Street; 415/981-7308), and **Pearl City** (641 Jackson Street; 415/398-8383).

The dim sum carts are constantly in motion, going from table to table so that diners can keep selecting items until they can't eat any more. In the old days, the bill was figured by counting the number of empty plates on the table. Now the waiters keep track (it's hard for one person to run up a tab of more than $10).

On most dim sum restaurant tables are cruets or bottles of chili oil, soy sauce, and vinegar, as well as Chinese mustard and other condiments for flavoring the different kinds of dim sum. Among the varieties you're most apt to encounter are:

Cha Siu So—flakey buns
Chun Guen—spring rolls
Chu Siu Bow—steamed barbecued pork buns

Dan Tar—custard tart
Floweret Siu Mai—meat-filled dumplings
Gee Cheung Fun—steamed rice noodle rolls
Gee Poke Go—pork triangles
Ha Gow—shrimp dumplings
Jow Ha Gok—shrimp turnovers
Kou Teh—pot-stickers with meat filling
Ngau Yuk Siu Mai—steamed meatballs
Siu Mai—steamed pork dumplings

French rolls are the base of Vietnamese sandwiches, but that's where any resemblance to American- or European-style sandwiches ends. First of all, they're less expensive. Second, though they may use the same meats and fish—sardines, meatballs, beef, barbecue pork, chicken, sausage, and turkey— they're joined by such ingredients as shredded carrots, cilantro, daikon, or other vegetables and smothered with lots of mayonnaise or other sandwich spread. The results are both tasty and filling.

Among the places where you can buy Vietnamese sandwiches are Irving Little Cafe and Sandwiches (2146 Irving Street; 415/681-2326), Saigon Sandwiches (560 Larkin Street; 415/474-5698), the Little Paris Coffee Shop (939 Stockton Street; 415/982-6111), and Tây Vîet (2034 Chestnut Street; 415/567-8124), where specialties include imperial rolls that are stuffed with mint and crabmeat.

---

and chairs provide a delightful ambience, at **Ti Couz** (3108 6th Street; 415/252-7373) the place to sit is at the counter. That way you can watch the restaurant's featured delicacies— crepes—being made. The dinner crepes are stuffed with ratatouille, salmon, Gruyère cheese, and a dozen other fillings, while the paper-thin dessert pancakes are paired with such sweet things as fresh berries or white chocolate and poached pears. Prices per crepe go from $1.95 to $5.25.

Also French is **Cafe Jacqueline** (1454 Grant Avenue; 415/981-5564) where there's a heavy emphasis on feather-light soufflés. In fact, other than a few soups and salads, they're the only items on the menu. Savory soufflés include black truffle and lobster, salmon and asparagus, white corn with ginger and garlic, and shitake mushroom. The chocolate souffle is the star of the sweets. While you're waiting, you can watch the chef and owner Jacqueline whipping up the eggs for the soufflés, which serve two to four people and cost between $25 and $50.

The Spanish equivalent of dim sum are tapas, appetizers that are great for people who want to make a meal of them. At **Alegrias** (2018 Lombard Street; 415/929-8888), tapas, which cost from $3 to $6 each, include mussels in garlic and wine, stewed tripe, garlicky shrimp, and crepes with apple filling. For your money, you also get live flamenco guitar music from Thursday to Saturday from 7:30 to 10 P.M. At **Sol y Luna** (475 Sacramento Street; 415/296-8696), tapas are even less expensive, starting at $2.50.

The upscale **Timo's Norte** menu (Ghirardelli Square, 900 North Point; 415/440-1200) lists twenty-five imaginative tapas, which include salt cod–potato cake with cilantro-mint salsa ($7.75), Spanish Cantimpalo and Soria chorizos (sausages; $3.75), and Catalan-style spinach with pine nuts, raisins, and apricots ($4.75). Tapas at **Zarzuela** (2000 Hyde Street; 415/346-0800) are also gourmet and include poached octopus and roast duck leg.

The decor isn't fancy at **Taiwan Restaurant** (445 Clement Street; 415/387-1789), but the food is terrific—try the crispy chicken, shanghai noodles, and turnip cakes for a meal that's different than the usual Chinese restaurant fare. Most meals cost less than $10 per person. **Ton Kiang** (5821 Geary Boulevard; 415/386-8530), with entrées from $7 to $15, focuses on Hakka-style main courses like fresh frog legs with ginger and asparagus as well as a variety of clay-pot dishes.

At the more expensive **Wu Kong** (101 Spear Street; 415/957-9300), Shanghai cuisine, including drunken chicken, shanghai dumplings, vegetarian goose, prawns, and pan-fried noodles is featured (entrées start at about $9 and go to $25).

Eliza's (1457 18th Street; 415/648-9999) isn't your typical Chinese restaurant. Tea is served in demitasse Wedgwood cups, and the food is presented on colorful Italian pottery. Best described as Chinese-California, dishes include a terrific celery salad, mango chicken, and sunflower beef. Despite all the sophistication, prices at Eliza's are reasonable, at about $6.50 to $8.95 a dish.

Tu Lan (8 6th Street; 415/626-0927) is definitely a hole-in-the-wall, with decor that leaves something to be desired. It's smokey, too, from the grill. But the food is what you go there for. Soups are great, and the servings huge. Almost any of the Vietnamese dishes on the menu are outstanding. Items range in price from about $3.75 to $6, so a complete dinner for two will cost less than $20.

La Vie (5830 Geary Boulevard; 415/668-8080) is a modest Vietnamese storefront restaurant, with entrées costing between $6.25 and $9.95. Five-spice roast chicken, Vietnamese crepes, and grilled prawns are among the house favorites.

Another Vietnamese restaurant you might want to try is the **Slanted Door** (584 Valencia Street; 415/861-8032), where appetizers include spring rolls in peanut sauce and entrée favorites are shrimp with glass noodles, chicken simmered in caramel sauce and ginger, stir-fried beans, and five-spice chicken. Two people can easily spend less than $20 on dinner, even with lichee ice cream for dessert.

At **Katia's** (600 5th Avenue; 415/668-9292), the decor is Russian tearoom style, with pots of African violets on the snow-white tablecloths. Entrées, which are in the $10 to $15 range, include *pozharski* (minced chicken patty), a beef stroganoff, piroshki, and stuffed cabbage. Russian tunes performed by an accordion player add to the atmosphere.

If you have never tasted Burmese food, **Irrawaddy** (1769 Lombard Street; 415/931-2830) will give you an excellent introduction, as the food is very well prepared. Among the house specials are ginger salad, sea bass steamed in banana leaves, and daikon soup. Entrée prices range from $5.75 to $14.95.

The specialty at **Tommaso Ristorante Italiano,** remembered by old-timers as **Lupo's** (1042 Kearny Street; 415/398-9696), is pizza—as it has been for at least half a century. Combinations of ingredients are almost limitless, and the sauce is homemade. For dessert, the cannoli gets good reviews.

Pane e Vino (3011 Steiner Street; 415/346-2111) serves country Italian fare in a classic brick and plaster setting. Centerpiece of the dining room is a long table decorated with a wheel of parmesan cheese, a prosciutto ham, and fresh vegetables, artfully arranged. The menu features polenta and pasta in several guises, gnocchi with roasted rabbit, and other hearty dishes ranging in price from about $8 to $18.

A totally different kind of Italian restaurant, **Il Fornaio** (1265 Battery Street; 415/986-0100), is not my favorite but everyone else seems to think it's fabulous. It's contemporary Italian, both in decor—with lots of glass—and cuisine. Each month a different region of Italy is featured. Pasta dishes start at about $7.50, and there are several entrées in the $12 to $15 range.

Moose's (1652 Stockton Street; 415/989-7800) menu is described as "American contemporary cuisine in the Italian and French traditions of the Mediterranean. Whatever it's called, the food, though somewhat pricey, is delicious. Specialties include morel-ricotta tortellini with asparagus and fava beans; Mediterranean fish soup; gnocchi with smoked salmon; a fish, citrus, and feta cheese salad; Sante Fe flan (flavored with anise), and chocolate pear tart. You'll probably be paying more than $15 per person for dinner, but the food and ambience make it a good value.

Suppenkuche (601 Hayes Street; 415/252-9289), with its scrubbed pine tables and steins of flowers, has become the favorite German restaurant of many San Franciscans who mourn the fact that the traditional downtown German restaurants aren't as good as they used to be. Items on the Suppenkuche menu are the traditional potato pancakes, pork

IRISH COFFEE—A SAN FRANCISCO TRADITION

On a dark and stormy night in 1952, so the story goes, Stanton Delaplane sat in the bar at Dublin Airport, talking to bartender Joe Sheridan. Sheridan whipped up a drink for the well-known San Francisco columnist—Irish whiskey, coffee, cream, and sugar—to drive away the chill.

Delaplane brought the recipe back to one of his favorite San Francisco haunts, the **Buena Vista Cafe** (2765 Hyde Street; 415/474-5044), where since that time more than twenty million Irish Coffees have been served.

---

loin, and spatzle, with some innovations, such as German ravioli. Prices are moderate for dinner, as are those for weekend brunch ($5 to $8.50), which features such dishes as pork sausages, muesli, and an Emperor's pancake with apple and plum preserves.

La Taqueria (2889 Mission Street; 415/285-7117) is a Mexican take-out restaurant with terra cotta floor, Mexican tile walls, and an open kitchen. But the tacos and fajitas are made as they're ordered and the salsa has a fresh taste. The quesadillas are tasty too, and prices are right, at less than $10 for enough food to satisfy the heartiest of eaters.

O'Reilly's Bar and Restaurant (622 Green Street; 415/989-6222) serves authentic Irish food in an authentic Irish pub and dining room, with wainscoting, cobblestone floors, and wonderful photos of Ireland on the walls. Cottage pie (ground beef, mashed potatoes, and cheese) costs $8.50. Steak and kidney pie is $12. Corned beef and cabbage is $10.75, and the fry-up of fish, chips, cockles, and mussels is $8.95.

Des Alpes Restaurant (732 Broadway; 415/391-4249) is one of the best values in The City, with a seven-course meal that's served family-style. As with all traditional Basque dinners, at least two kinds of meat are served—such as sweetbreads, oxtail stew, lamb, trout, or steaks—along with tureens of soup, platters of mashed potatoes or french fries, and green salad. There's dessert, too.

At the **Original Cuba Restaurant** (2886 16th Street; 415/255-0946), specialties include seafood served on a bed of *congri* and the traditional Cuban combination of red beans, rice, and bacon. **Nambantei of Tokyo** (115 Cyril Magnin Street; 415/421-2101) has the reputation of being the most authentic yakitori (skewered and grilled bits of meat and fish) restaurant in San Francisco, and **Indian Oven** (233 Fillmore Street; 415/626-1628) is a good place to try traditional East Indian dishes that have been given a California twist.

Visitors who happen to be in town during an **ethnic festival** won't want to miss out on the food served at them. At the Russian festivals you'll find pierogi and *blini*; at Japanese celebrations, tempura, teriyaki, and bean buns. At the Norway Day festival in May (at Fort Mason), you can feast on *lefse* (the Norwegian version of a tortilla, only served with butter and sugar), open face sandwiches, *krumkage* (cylindrical waferlike cookies), and a variety of fancy cookies.

The October German celebration at Union Square is the time for sausages and strudel, and that same month it's focaccia, cannoli, and capuccino at North Beach's Italian festival.

The Trendies

People in the know say that Morton's, Lulu, and Grand Cafe are three of *the* places where everybody who is anybody (or hopes to be someday) goes. If you must have a steak and don't care what it costs, those at **Morton's of Chicago** (400 Post Street; 415/986-5830) have the reputation of being the best just about anywhere. The tenderloin brochette, the cheapest beef on the menu, costs $19.95. Rib-eyes are $23.95; the double filet mignon with bearnaise sauce is $27.95, and porterhouse or strip steaks are $29.95. And that's just for the meat. Side dishes are extra ($4.75 to $6.95).

Prices at **Restaurant Lulu** (816 Folsom Street; 415/495-5775) are easier on the wallet, though the noise level can be hard on the ears (that's why you'll see personnel wearing headphones). The warehouse interior features skylights and an open kitchen with wood-fired rotisserie. Menu choices range from calamari pizza with basil and aioli ($8.95) to pork loin with fennel and olive oil ($11.50). The more exotic grilled quail with balsamic vinegar, roasted onions, figs, pancetta, and arugula salad is $16.95. Appetizers and desserts are imaginative too (try the lemon tart).

The **Grand Cafe** (501 Geary Street; 415/292-0101) is located at Hotel Monaco in what was formerly a ballroom. With thirty-foot ceilings and an eclectic array of decorative touches—plush velvet booths, eight murals ranging in style from expressionist to fauvism, contemporary sculpture, terrazzo floors, massive art deco glass and brass chandeliers, huge pilasters, trompe l'oeil mosaic panels, and an exhibition kitchen with wood-burning stove reflected in a enormous art nouveau–style mirror—the restaurant is one you'll remember for years.

The food is described as California bistro–style, and includes such appetizers as puffy shrimp and scallop beignets with remoulade sauce. Entrées include chicken breast stuffed with mushroom duxelle and pinot noir sauce, and lobster and shrimp ravioli with julienne vegetables and lobster sorrel sauce. Appetizer prices go from $4.95 to $9.95, and entrées $9.95 to $16.

In the bar, which is separated from the dining room by a sculpture that nearly reaches the ceiling, less expensive fare is served. Menu items include a steak sandwich with grilled vegetables and aioli, pizzas from the wood-burning oven, and lemon crème brulée.

For people willing to take a gamble, the two restaurants at

the **California Culinary Academy** (625 Polk Street; 415/771-3500) are worth a try. Staffed by cooking school students under the watchful eyes of their instructors, results can range from weird to wonderful. At the less formal Grill Room, there's a grill buffet from Monday through Thursday from 6 to 9 P.M. that costs just $9.95 per person ($11.95 for the Friday night prime rib buffet).

More creative cookery is featured in the Careme Room, where lunch costs $12.95, and dinner $17.95. Though reservations are required for the Careme Room, they're not necessary for the Grill.

People who follow the "Let's find a place that looks good" technique of restaurant selection will do well to head for Clement Street in the Richmond District. There, during a five-minute stroll, you'll find Chinese, French, Japanese, Russian, Thai, and Vietnamese restaurants. To reach the Richmond District from Union Square, take the no. 38 Geary bus.

Delicatessen Dining

Most San Francisco delis have a few tables and chairs where you can consume their sandwiches and salads. If they don't, there's usually a park, bench, or wall nearby where you can picnic. Almost every delicatessen—even those in super-markets—features freshly made sandwiches and good-quality products. We've narrowed our choices down to five, based on their reputations for excellence.

Panelli Brothers Delicatessen (1419 Stockton Street; 415/421-2541) and **Molinari Delicatessen** (373 Columbus Avenue; 415/421-2337) are two North Beach establishments of long standing. Great wheels of parmesan cheese, salamis hanging from the ceiling, hunks of prosciutto, imported mushrooms, and olive oils create the decor and an aroma that's divine. The house-made salads, antipasti, breads, meats, and cheese are the stuff memorable al fresco meals are made of.

Moishe's Pippic (425-A Hayes Street; 415/431-2440) is, according to the locals, the current front-runner as far as Jewish delicatessens are concerned. Chicago-style, its specialties include pastrami, hot dogs, and chopped liver sandwiches. More conveniently located as far as most hotels are concerned, **David's Delicatessen** (474 Geary Street; 415/771-1600) has for years been famous for its Reubens, blintzes, and soups. As far as I'm concerned, it's a great place to sit at the counter and have a bowl of matzo ball soup before going to the theater or symphony (there's also an adjoining room for more formal meals).

Moscow and Tbilisi Bakery (5540 Geary Boulevard; 415/668-6959; carries typical Russian items, such as pickled vegetables, pickled tomatoes, piroshki, and cream puffs.

Miscellaneous Munch-Rooms

For people who don't want to miss a moment of vacation fun but are desperate for clean clothes, it's **Brain Wash Cafe and Laundromat** at 1122 Folsom Street (415/861-FOOD or 431-WASH). You can wash your clothes in a Maytag twelve-pounder for $1.50 a load or a Wascomat twenty-five pounder ($2.50) if you have a lot of them. If you really want to live it up, you can have an attendant wash and fold your clothes for 80¢ a pound. Soap is 40¢ a cup, and the dryer costs 25¢ for eight minutes.

While you're separating the whites from the colors or the clothes are sloshing around, you can order from a menu that includes soup ($2.85), salads ($4.75 to $7.50), sandwiches ($4.95 to $7.25), meat loaf ($7.25), fish and chips ($5.95), and a Middle Eastern vegetarian plate ($6.95).

If you can't make it for lunch or dinner, breakfast is served weekdays from 8 to 11 A.M., and even longer on weekends. If you're not interested in eating, you can choose from an array of coffees, beers, wine, or other beverages while you listen to DJs or live entertainment in the evening (it's rumored that the performers get to do free loads), play the pinball machines, or cozy up to the San Francisco computer on-line terminal.

For more focus on the Internet, you may choose to ignore the laundry and eat at one of the several new **computer-connected restaurants** that have appeared on the San Francisco dining scene since the surf-the-net craze began. Two of them are **Cyberworld** (528 Folsom Street; 415/278-9669), where California cuisine is served, and **Internet Alfredo** (790-A Brannan Street; 415/437-3140) with emphasis on Italian food. There's also the **Internet Coffee House**, at 744 Harrison Street (415/495-7447).

The "Preferred Dining in San Francisco With Visa" promotion, in effect during the latter part of 1996 until April 1997, is the kind of program to be on the lookout for. Under the plan, Visa cardholders could take advantage of complimentary desserts or appetizers, priority table reservations, discounts of 20 percent, or two-for-one meals at the more than 150 Bay Area restaurants that participated, simply by calling a toll-free number to obtain a preferred diner's card.

A newsletter containing short descriptions of participating restaurants was sent to members along with the membership card, which had to be shown when ordering. Visa cards also had to be used to pay for the meals in order to qualify for the specials. Among the restaurants included were the Grand Cafe, John's Grill, Lulu, Tandoori Mahal, and Vanessi's Nob Hill.

While you're at the visitor center, grab every restaurant brochure you can find that includes a discount coupon. It's silly to eat at a place merely because you can get a deal, but it frequently turns out that you just happen to have a coupon for a restaurant that appeals to you. For example, the Veranda, on the second floor of the Crowne Plaza Parc 55, often has a 10 percent discount coupon in circulation. The restaurant is very pleasant (try to get a window table looking out on the street), and the food is excellent.

You'll find coupons and information on discounted deals in

magazines and newspapers, too. For example, in the March/ April 1997 issue of *VIA*, the magazine of the California AAA, an item reported that diners showing their AAA membership cards at any Hard Rock Cafe in the United States prior to ordering would receive a 10 percent discount on all food and beverages. The **Hard Rock Cafe** in San Francisco is at 1699 Van Ness Avenue (415/885-1699).

Parking near most San Francisco restaurants is difficult, if not impossible, and valet parking, where available, is usually expensive. You'll save money and your temper by taking public transportation or a cab.

Since hours and closing days vary—as do the credit cards accepted—it's a good idea to phone ahead to make reservations and have any uncertainties clarified.

Free Lunch?

If you can wait until five o'clock to have lunch or only want a bite for dinner, take advantage of Happy Hours at San Francisco bars. Some of them cost only the price of a drink.

At the bar of the **Buchanan Grill** (3653 Buchanan Street; 415/346-8727), free hot dogs are served during football season from 5 to 7 P.M. Little sandwiches with a variety of fillings are free during Happy Hour the rest of the year.

Free hors d'oeuvres at **City of Paris** (550 Geary Street; 415/441-4442) include onion rings, cold cuts, and little crab cakes from Monday to Friday, 5 to 7 P.M.

You'll have to pay $5 plus a one-drink minimum (drink prices start at less than $3) at the Hurricane Bar of the Fairmont Hotel's Tonga Restaurant. In return, you'll get your drink plus all you can eat of eight different kinds of hors d'oeuvres, including filling dishes like chow mein.

Some restaurants, such as New Joe's, feature a free dish every day—like pizza or spaghetti—a custom that goes back to The City's barrooms during Gold Rush days.

One final word of gustatory advice. You can even save as

you splurge. For example, at **Fleur de Lys** (777 Sutter Street; 415/673-7779), you can spend hundreds of dollars on a dinner for two if you order à la carte and choose only moderately priced wines (entrées range from about $26 to $34). Even at those prices there's a great deal of value received for money spent, as owner and chef Hubert Keller consistently makes the lists of the ten finest chefs in the country.

However, you can have the restaurant's exquisite food and romantic ambience (the centerpiece of the room is a large tentlike construction of flowered fabric highlighting an impressive floral arrangement) for far less if you select one of the least expensive wines and order either the four-course regular tasting menu ($65) or the four-course vegetarian tasting menu ($52).

While the menus change with the season and the availability of fresh foods, typical dishes for the regular tasting menu include a sampling of appetizers, maybe American fois gras, a quinoa lobster nugget, and sautéed crab cake. The appetizers are followed by a fish course—perhaps Atlantic salmon—followed by herb-crusted lamb rack or black pepper encrusted filet mignon. (A second fish dish, such as seared ahi tuna, can be substituted for the meat course.) The fourth course might be chocolate crème brulée, followed by petit fours and coffee or tea.

CHAPTER

4

Going Places

Look at a map of San Francisco and you'll realize that it is an extremely compact city. Surrounded by water on three sides and connected on the south to a series of peninsular communities stretching all the way to San Jose and beyond, The City covers an area of only forty-six or forty-seven square miles, depending upon whose measurements you go by. As a result, most of the sights, attractions, activities, shopping, and dining that will interest you are located in a relatively small area.

Although residents may tell you otherwise, San Francisco actually does have an excellent transportation system when compared to most other cities. Commuters arrive via auto, bus, train, BART (Bay Area Rapid Transit), and even by ferryboat. Once in The City, they travel on foot and by San Francisco Municipal Railway (Muni) streetcars, buses, or cable cars to their workplaces. For the tourist, this public transportation translates into big savings, for one of the expenses that's easiest to control is that of getting from place to place.

The majority of San Francisco's sixteen million annual visitors arrive by car. This can prove to be a money-saver (if someone in your party is adept at driving The City's roller-coaster hills and you have an inexpensive or free place to park while you're in town). But having an automobile in San Francisco also can be a money-gulper. Daily parking rates at downtown hotels tend toward the horrendous ($20 is not

CURB COLORS

If you have any doubt as to whether you can legally park, don't do it. San Francisco may well have the most stringently enforced on-street parking code in the United States of America. As a result, if you don't pay attention to the colors painted on curbs that signify various parking regulations, chances are you'll get caught. And that means you'll pay. Plenty.

Parking tickets cost at least $20. And that doesn't include towing ($100) and hefty storage fees. The fine for parking illegally in a bus zone or wheelchair access space is $250, while blocking access to a wheelchair ramp can cost you $275. Getting your car released can be a time-consuming process, too. Colors of the various reserved parking zones are:

Red—no stopping or parking
Yellow—half-hour limit loading for vehicles with
    commercial plates only
Yellow and Black—half-hour loading for trucks with
    commercial plates only
Green, Yellow, and Black—taxi zone
Blue—disabled parking with license plate or placard
Green—ten-minute parking for all vehicles
White—five-minute limit for all vehicles during adjacent
    businesses' hours of operation

Be aware, too, that on-street parking in various neighborhoods is by permit only. These areas are posted, but it's easy to miss the signs if you don't know that they exist.

It is also the law that drivers must curb their wheels when parking on San Francisco hills. Just turn the tires toward the street when facing uphill, and toward the curb when facing downhill. That way the curb will act as a block in case your parking brakes fail to hold on the steep grades.

Even though commercial parking garages in the downtown area are expensive, you'll save potential headaches by using them—even when on-street parking is available—if there's any question about being able to get back to your vehicle in the allotted time. Among the larger parking facilities are:

Downtown:
  833 Mission Street; 415/982-8522
  Mason and Ellis; 415/771-1400
  Ellis and O'Farrell, 123 O'Farrell; 415/986-4800
  Union Square, 333 Post Street; 415/397-0631
  Sutter and Stockton; 415/982-8370
  Civic Center, 370 Grove Street; 415/626-4484
  Embarcadero Center; 415/398-1878
  250 Clay Street; 415/433-4722
  Moscone Center/Yerba Buena Gardens—255 Third Street;
    415/777-2782
  Museum Parc, 3rd and Folson; 415/543-4533
Fisherman's Wharf:
  665 Beach at Hyde; 415/673-5197
Japan Center:
  1660 Geary Boulevard; 415/567-4573
Union Street:
  1910 Laguna; 415/563-9820
  2055 Lombard Street; 415/495-3772

Expect to pay about $3.75 to $4.50 an hour at Fisherman's Wharf. However, there's a $10 maximum, so for stays of several hours the per hour cost isn't terrific ($15 Monday to Friday overnight; $18 Saturday and Sunday overnight). Charges at the Union Square Garage are $1 for each half hour for the first six hours; six to twenty-four hours, $20. That means if you park for six hours and fifteen minutes you'll have to pay the same as for twenty-four hours. The garage at Japan Center has among the best rates in town, at $1 an hour and $10 for 24-hour parking. However, unless you're staying there, the garage's location isn't practical for most visitors.

One last admonition: Remember that in California, pedestrians always have the right of way.

---

unusual) and fees for parking in public garages near the city center are also high.

Experts advise people who plan to travel to San Francisco by car to obtain a map in advance (see chapter 13, Sources and

Resources) and study it so that you have the route to your hotel figured out. As an additional help, jot down on a piece of paper (in large letters you can easily read) the names of the streets you must take in sequential order. Time your arrival and departure so that you miss rush hour (roughly 7 to 9 A.M. and 4 to 6 P.M.). Traffic going out of The City can also be horrific on Friday afternoons, especially when the weather is fine. Once you've arrived at your hotel, park your car and rely on public transportation except for out-of-town excursions.

Getting To and From the Airport

If you travel on one of the 1,260 flights that arrive each day at San Francisco International Airport—the world's seventh busiest—the first transportation you'll need will be to your hotel, motel, or other lodging place. A taxi usually costs about $35 to $55, depending on passengers' destinations and traffic conditions. With four people sharing, the per person cost gives you convenience and comfort without breaking the bank. But if one person's paying the tab plus the tip from his or her own pocket, it's another story.

Three airporter bus lines operate to and from San Francisco. SFO Airporter has two routes. Route 1 (Union Square) stops at the ANA Hotel, Grand Hyatt, Westin St. Francis, Hilton, Nikko, Crowne Plaza Parc 55, and the Mariott. Route 2 (Downtown) stops at the Hyatt Regency, Sheraton Palace, Holiday Inn, Westin St. Francis, Hilton, Nikko, and Mariott. As a result, there are trips every fifteen minutes between the airport and hotels served by both routes; every thirty minutes between the others. The full-size buses operate from 5 A.M. to midnight. Fare is $10 from the airport to The City for both adults and children; $9 from The City to the airport.

Pacific Airporter's Route A buses stop at the Moscone Center, Howard Johnson Pickwick Hotel, Savoy, Bedford, Pan Pacific, Maxwell (formerly the Rafael), Vintage Court, King George, and Holiday Civic Center. Hotel stops on Route B are the California, Cartwright, Sheehan, Canterbury, Fairmont, Mark Hopkins, Stanford Court, Ritz Carlton, Holiday Inn Financial District, and Park Hyatt. The one-way adult fare is $9, round-trip $15 (children $6 and $10). Discount coupons are often available. Buses leave every half hour.

The Wharf Airporter stops at Howard Johnson, Ramada Plaza Hotel, Travelodge Hotel, the Sheraton, Hyatt, Holiday Inn, and Mariott—all at Fisherman's Wharf—the Comfort Inn, Holiday Inn–Golden Gateway, Richelieu–Cathedral Hill, and the Opera House. Adult fares are $10 one way; $16 round-trip. Youngsters 10 to 15 ride for half fare, and there's no charge for children under 10. The buses run every thirty minutes from 5 A.M. until 10 P.M.

Several **shuttle services** offer door-to-door drop-off and pickup, an especially important feature when you're staying somewhere outside the tourist district. Among them are:

SuperShuttle (700 16th Street; 415/558-8500 and 415/871-7800) offers 24-hour service to and from SFO, San Francisco, and the South Bay Peninsula. Fares are about $11 one-way, with reduced fares for additional people in the same party.

Quake City Shuttle, 415/255-4899; Bay Shuttle, 415/564-3400; and American Airporter Shuttle, 415/546-6689 are among the services that charge $10 per person but offer fare-reduction coupons in the *Bay City Guide* and other free publications.

Travelers with luggage that can fit on their laps or on the floor by their feet can take the 3B or 3X SamTrans bus to the BART station at Colma (a fourteen-minute ride that costs $1) and then transfer to any of the trains to downtown. The BART ride will take between sixteen and twenty minutes, depending on your destination, and costs $1.80. Trains leave every seven to fifteen minutes.

SamTrans buses run between the airport and downtown San Francisco approximately every half hour, and the trip usually takes from twenty-two to thirty minutes, depending on traffic. Tickets cost $2.50. Stops at 7th and Mission streets and 1st and Mission are within easy walking distance to many downtown hotels. However, you're only allowed a briefcase or tote bag if you ride the express buses.

The very least expensive way to go between the airport and downtown San Francisco takes longer but costs just $1.75. Free shuttles run between the airport and the Millbrae CalTrain station. The problem with this scheme is that while you're saving a little bit of money you may spend a good deal of time, since trains don't run as frequently as the buses, except during commute hours. Also, the CalTrain terminal is at 4th and Townsend streets, a fair walk from most hotels.

If you want to ride in style, Celebrity Limousine (415/990-9072 or 982-5466) advertises a bargain $35 rate from the airport to San Francisco for up to four people, but reservations must be made in advance. At present, no limousines operate from the airport without advance reservations.

Pickup Points

The airport, located about fourteen miles south of The City, is composed of the South, International, and North terminals, which are joined by enclosed walkways. Buses depart from the airport's lower level outside the baggage claim areas at the blue column on the center island of each terminal. Schedules and fares are posted at these points.

Shuttles stop on the upper level center islands outside the airline ticket counters at all terminals. Specifics on fares and areas serviced are posted and also are available at the information booths inside the airport.

Bus stops on the upper level at the International and North terminals serve public transportation vehicles, including regular SamTrans buses to and from the airport and San Francisco, the CalTrain–SFO Shuttle, and the BART–SFO Express. Schedules and fares are posted at the bus stops.

You can also get information regarding transportation, including schedules and fares, at information booths in the various terminals and at computerized kiosks located in the baggage claim areas.

Oakland Arrivals

If you have arrived across the bay at Oakland International Airport (See chapter 1, Pretrip Prep), you can get to downtown San Francisco most economically by taking a shuttle bus to the Coliseum–Oakland International Airport BART station ($2, adults; 50¢ children 13 and under, the handicapped, and seniors over 60; exact change required) and a BART train to one of the downtown stations ($2.45). AirBART shuttles leave the center island outside the airport every fifteen minutes from 6 A.M. to midnight, Monday to Saturday, and 8:30 A.M. to midnight on Sunday (holiday schedules vary).

During the day, take the Daly City–Colma train and get off at the San Francisco BART station (Embarcadero, Montgomery, Powell, or Civic Center) closest to your destination. Trains run every fifteen minutes and the ride takes between nineteen and twenty-four minutes. There is no direct service to San Francisco from the Coliseum Station after 7:31 P.M., Monday to Friday, or 6:34 P.M. Saturday or Sunday, when you must take a Richmond train and transfer to a Daly City–Colma train at Oakland's 12th Street Station.

When your accommodations aren't within walking distance of a BART station, a shuttle directly to your destination will be your least expensive option. Among the shuttle companies that operate between Oakland International and San Francisco are:

A-1 Shuttle ($12 to $40)	510/676-0565
Bayporter Express ($13 to $42)	800/287-6783
City Express ($12 to $25)	888/874-8885
Luxor Shuttle ($10 to $25)	510/562-7222
SuperShuttle ($12 to $21)	510/268-8700

America's Shuttle ($16; 415/515-0273 and 510/841-0272)

stops only at the Bedford and Juliana hotels, Monticello Inn, Hotel Sir Francis Drake, and Villa Florence.

Taxis cost the same as they do from San Francisco International (about $35 to $55). Traffic during morning commute hours can make this a long ride from either airport. Although driving time to San Francisco may be longer from Oakland than San Francisco International, the former airport is so much smaller that the time from plane to baggage carousel to curbside is usually much shorter.

Amtrak also serves the Bay Area (arriving in Oakland) from the north, east, and south. Greyhound buses arrive at and leave from the Transbay Transit Terminal at 425 Market Street, between 1st and Fremont streets.

Travelers who arrive in the Bay Area by plane, Amtrak, or bus—especially those combining business with pleasure or those who want to go on excursions outside The City—may find it convenient to rent a car for part of their stays. Whether or not it's a money-saver will depend on the size of their group, the places they plan to go within San Francisco and its environs, and the parking fees they incur. Among the larger car rental agencies, many of which have toll-free numbers, are:

Agency Rent-A-Car	800/321-1972
Alamo	800/327-9633
Allstate Car Rental	800/634-6186
Avis Rent-A-Car	800/831-2847
Budget Car and Truck Rental	800/527-0700
Dollar Rent-A-Car	800/800-4000
Enterprise Rent-A-Car	800/325-8007
Hertz	800/654-3131
Lloyd's International Rent-A-Car	800/654-7037
National Car Rental	800/CAR-RENT
Payless Car Rental	800/PAYLESS
Thrifty Car Rental	800/367-2277
Value Rent-A-Car	800/GO-VALUE

In addition, there are dozens of other operations. The cost of car rentals can vary so widely—not only from season to season but from one rental agency to another—that it pays to shop around. However, if they don't have toll-free numbers, when you make numerous phone calls you may spend more than you save.

Since San Francisco hosts a large number of conventions each year and car rates go up with increased demand, it is difficult to predict when rentals will be the least expensive.

To be sure you get your money's worth, ask the following questions: Are any unadvertised discounts available? What are the additional charges for taxes (are agencies with offices at the airport subject to higher taxes than those with off-airport locations)? What other factors can increase the base price? There may be booking requirements for the lowest rates, such as making the reservation a day or more in advance; for additional drivers; driving in California-only restrictions, or drop-off charges if you want to pick the car up at the airport and turn it in at a downtown location.

You'll want to check the information you gather against the prices you've seen quoted in newspaper travel and entertainment sections, airline in-flight magazines, and any discount coupons you may have collected.

If you're going to be in San Francisco at the same time a big convention or trade show is taking place, you might not be able to rent *any* car unless you reserve months in advance. By contrast, if your visit coincides with a slow or even moderately busy time of year, shopping around can save you a good deal of money.

The Streets of San Francisco

Whether or not you have a car at your disposal, it will usually make economic sense and save wear and tear on your nerves to take public transportation. Taxi rates vary from company to company, but are typically $1.70 for the first mile and $1.80 for each additional mile. Hailing a cab during rush hour or on a rainy night can be nearly impossible, however. At any time, if you aren't close to a taxi stand, your best bet is to have the hotel doorman or restaurant maitre d' call one for you.

Cabs are generally impractical for transportation to locations such as the zoo and other attractions in outlying parts of The City, but there may be times when the only way to get where you want to go is by taxi. Even then you can save money by timing your trips so they don't coincide with rush hours. You will also want to use a taxi when you're going off the beaten track after dark, especially if you are traveling alone.

A Ticket to Ride

Individual **Municipal Railway** rides by bus or streetcar in The City cost $1, and include transfers. One-way cable car rides cost $2. If you plan to do a lot of traveling by bus and cable car, it may pay to buy a pocket-size Muni Passport. These entitle their bearers to unlimited rides on buses and cable cars, cost $6 for one day, $10 for three consecutive days, and $15 for seven consecutive days.

The cable car, it's claimed, is the only mode of transportation in the United States that is also a national landmark. Invented by Andrew Hallidie in the early 1870s, the cable car system was inaugurated in August 1873. At their pre-1906 height, more than 110 miles of cable pulled more than five hundred cars along eight tracks. Today only three routes remain. The Powell-Hyde Line follows a route along Powell, Washington, and Hyde streets to Victorian Park near Fort Mason, Ghirardelli Square, the Cannery, and Aquatic Park. The Powell-Mason Line goes from the cable car turnaround at Powell and Market streets to Bay Street, which is a couple of blocks from Fisherman's Wharf. A shorter route, the California Line, runs between Embarcadero Center and California Street, climbing over Nob Hill on its way.

From 1917 to 1928, San Francisco put into place an extensive streetcar system, complete with five different lines and two tunnels that made it possible to develop the windswept dunes beyond the hills in The City's western reaches. Unlike most metropolitan areas after World War II, San Francisco defied the national trend to pull up tracks and stop streetcar service. As a result, the streetcar lines were converted to a light rail system between 1980 and 1982. In combination with Muni buses and cable cars, these light rail buses (still referred to by everyone as streetcars) make it possible to go to within a block or so of most San Francisco attractions.

For example, the N-Judah streetcar line goes from downtown out Judah Street to about a block from the beach. Line L-Taraval runs along Market Street like all the other lines and terminates at 46th Avenue and Wawona Street about a mile and a half south of the N-Judah Line. Line M–Ocean View cuts through the Castro, Twin Peaks, and West Portal districts to south of Stonestown Galleria at Taraval. K-Ingleside follows essentially the same route, but branches off to serve the Ingleside neighborhood. Line J-Church begins at Embarcadero Center, goes down Market Street, then runs down Church Street past Mission Dolores to 24th Street.

Bus no. 15 cuts through Chinatown and North Beach, but no. 38 goes right past Japan Center, and bus no. 42 runs between the eastern edge of downtown and the Fisherman's Wharf area. Streetcar and bus stops are identified by pole signs, street markings, or yellow bands painted on adjacent utility poles.

Four San Francisco BART stops—Civic Center, Powell Street, Montgomery Street, and Embarcadero—allow passengers to go from place to place downtown in just a matter of minutes. The 16th Avenue and 24th Avenue stops in the Mission District are near popular tourist destinations, too—Mission Dolores and the Precita Eyes Mural Art Center (see chapter 6, Neighborhoods and Ethnic Enclaves).

Before you set out to visit an attraction, study the time schedule and map booklet to see which route will get you there most efficiently. You can also get information from bus drivers, especially if the buses aren't crowded.

Two-Wheelers

If you've brought your bike along, it will serve you well when you visit such places as Golden Gate Park, posh residential districts such as Sea Cliff, and points outside of San Francisco (see chapters 11 and 12, on trips and excursions). Riding bicycles downtown, however, is hazardous.

Renting a bike is a rather expensive proposition. The going rate is $4 to $5 an hour and $20 to $25 for a full day. You'll find coupons for varying amounts off the day rates in the free weekly and monthly publications available at visitor information centers, as well as at hotel concierge and bell desks. However, during the winter season, when rates are at their lowest, these coupons may not be accepted at some businesses.

When you plan to stay in the Bay Area a week or more and expect to ride frequently, consider buying a used bicycle at a thrift shop or secondhand store and then selling it when you're ready to leave for home. Be sure, however, that the bike you buy is in rideable condition and the price is less than the $105 weekly rental rate you would otherwise have to pay.

Some of the businesses that rent bicycles are:

American Rentals, 2715 Hyde Street; 415/931-0234; $5 an hour, $25 for a full day includes a helmet, map, and a lock.

Blazing Saddles Bike Rental, 1095 Columbus; 415/202-8888; $5 an hour, $25 for a full day. Rental fees include helmets, locks, bike bags, maps, and bottle cages.

Golden Gate Rentals, 990 Columbus Avenue; 415/351-1188; $4 an hour, $23 per day. Advertises free pickup from any location in The City, with minimum two-hour rental. Skate rentals are also available if you want to go rollerblading down the streets of San Francisco.

Holiday Adventures, 1937 Lombard Street; 415/567-1192; $5 an hour, $20 per day includes helmets, locks, saddlebags, and maps.

There also are clusters of bicycle rental facilities along Stanyan, Haight, and Fulton streets near Golden Gate Park.

Pedestrian Power

The least expensive of all transportation modes—walking—works very well in the central part of town, and even farther afield if you don't mind climbing a hill now and then. If you're staying downtown, you'll soon realize that many of the major attractions and several of the ethnic districts are within easy walking distance.

It's important, however, for walkers to realize that San Francisco is like other big cities with a large transient population. It's not a good idea to go walking in the Tenderloin (the twenty-square-block area west of Union Square roughly bounded by Taylor, Polk, O'Farrell, and Golden Gate streets) or in some areas south of Market Street after dark.

Strangely enough, unsafe neighborhoods frequently abut those that are upscale, i.e., the Tenderloin is next to elegant Nob Hill and the Western Addition is near posh Pacific Heights. If you have any questions regarding an area's safety, inquire at the hotel desk before you venture forth.

Wherever you go, take precautions such as carrying wallets in inside pockets, securely hanging on to purses (or better yet, not carrying them), and not wearing a good deal of expensive jewelry.

Water Transport

Although you can only go between two points in San Francisco via ferry (Pier 39 to the Ferry Building), the boats are a form of transportation that shouldn't be missed. (You'll find out more about the ferryboats in the sight-seeing and excursions chapters.)

CHAPTER
5
Shopping and Souvenir Specials

San Francisco is one of America's great shopping bazaars. Whether you have a platinum card with unlimited credit or wallet containing only a modest amount of cash, the City by the Bay's array of merchandise won't disappoint you—especially if you're looking for bargains.

You'll find opportunities to spend your money all over town. Many of The City's top stores—Macy's, Neiman-Marcus, and Saks Fifth Avenue among them—front on Union Square or the streets radiating from it. Unlike downtown areas in many large cities, San Francisco's commercial center has remained vibrant and full of vitality through the years.

A trio of major shopping centers are located downtown. There are shopping malls and festival marketplaces in outlying places like Fisherman's Wharf, and streets that have become famous for their interesting shops and boutiques. Here's a rundown of those to look for. Some of them are pricey, while others are a bargain-hunter's paradise. All of them will make born-again shoppers wish they had planned longer trips.

San Francisco Shopping Center (865 Market Street; 415/495-5656), located across from the downtown Powell Street cable car turnaround, is a nine-level vertical mall with

America's only spiral escalators to take shoppers from one floor to another. The top five levels are occupied by the world's largest Nordstrom department store, while the lower levels contain ninety retail businesses—most of them upscale.

Crocker Galleria's (50 Post Street; 415/393-1505) spectacular glass dome is reason enough to step inside this shopping center. Not far from Union Square, it's modeled after Milan's enormous Galleria Vittorio Emmanuelle. The three-level pavilion features forty upscale boutiques and two rooftop gardens that are ideal for warm weather relaxing and picnicking.

Embarcadero Center (Embarcadero at Market Street; 800/733-6318 or 415/772-0500) is a sprawling shopping area along the waterfront that covers eight city blocks. More than 125 shops and restaurants, plus a movie complex and two major hotels, are part of the center, where the big drawback is difficulty in finding the shop you're looking for. The Embarcadero Center's open spaces are popular venues for outdoor entertainment.

Away From the City Center

Stonestown Galleria, with its vaulted glass skylights and Italian renaissance marble, is located in San Francisco's Sunset District, at 19th Avenue and Winston Drive (415/759-2626). Though the shopping complex dates back to the 1950s, it has been periodically spruced up and is a pleasant place to shop. Its bonus is free outside parking. It's also accessible by taking the M streetcar line.

Ghirardelli Square (900 North Point Street; 415/775-5500) is both charming and historically interesting. Domenico "Domingo" Ghirardelli, of Rapallo, Italy, came to San Francisco in 1849 and in 1865 discovered how to manufacture "broma," the ground chocolate for which he became famous. In 1885, he and his sons purchased an entire city block of property overlooking the San Francisco Bay, which served as the company's manufacturing facility and headquarters. In 1964, Ghirardelli Square was completely renovated, and since that time has been one of San Francisco's favorite shopping spots.

With more than seventy shops and restaurants, the marketplace offers fabulous views of the bay, beautifully landscaped gardens, and a self-guided walking tour of its buildings. And for a taste of history, you may want to stop at the **Ghirardelli Chocolate Manufactory** on the first floor for a hot fudge sundae. The square, which is on the National Historic Register, is bounded by North Point, Polk, Beach, and Larkin streets, and is about one block from the Powell-Hyde Line cable car turnaround at the bay.

Another landmark, the ivy-covered **Cannery** (2801 Leavenworth Street; 415/771-3112) was built in 1907 as a fruit and vegetable canning plant. The imposing brick complex, which opened in 1967 as a shopping center, contains about two dozen shops and galleries in addition to restaurants and cafes, a museum, a comedy club, and a TV station. Three levels of walkways, bridges, and balconies surround the flower-filled courtyard with its picnic benches and one-hundred-year-old olive trees. The area's best street entertainers often perform at Ghirardelli Square and the Cannery.

Pier 39 (Beach Street and Embarcadero (415/981-PIER), a festival marketplace with more than one hundred shops, offers some of the best views of The City and is a favorite with youngsters (see chapter 8, Sights Worth Seeing, and chapter 10, Family Planning). Pier 39 is located two blocks east of Fisherman's Wharf.

The **Anchorage** at Fisherman's Wharf (415/775-6000) is decorated with hundreds of multicolored signal flags and a twenty-seven-foot anchor entrance. The one-block shopping area, bounded by Leavenworth, Jefferson, Beach, and Jones streets, is one block from the Hyde Street cable car turnaround.

CHECKOUT TIME COST-CUTTERS

• Store personnel cannot charge customers an extra fee for using credit cards. They may, however, offer discounts for cash purchases. Be sure to ask.

• Some of the larger department stores offer a 10 percent day-long discount to shoppers who open a charge account with them. If you're making a significant purchase, you might take advantage of this savings even if you don't use the card again.

• A sales tax of 8.5 percent is charged on every item unless the customer has it shipped outside of California. In some cases, shipping costs can cancel out the tax savings, but if you purchase relatively high-cost items that don't weigh a lot, consider having them sent to your home.

Japan Center (at 941 Geary Boulevard, bounded by Geary, Laguna, Fillmore, and Post streets; 415/922-6776) is the focal point of The City's Japanese cultural activities and business life. The center houses a deluxe hotel, banks, a movie theater, Japanese-style baths and markets, restaurants, and shops. (To get to the Japan Center from downtown, take the 38 Geary bus.)

Best known of the shopping avenues is **Union Street** in Cow Hollow. Outer Sacramento Street near Presidio Avenue offers a smaller cluster of boutiques, galleries, coffeehouses, and restaurants. Chestnut and Clement streets are also known for their shops. The number 45-Union bus will get you to the shops from downtown.

Discount and Outlet Shopping

The South of Market area of San Francisco has been home to its **garment district** for decades. Therefore, when the discount phenomena became a way of American shopping life, it was no surprise that discount stores would open near their sources of supply. Clothing outlets have been joined by discount operations handling housewares, furniture, and gifts, so that now there are more than one-hundred of these bargain centers in The City.

Georgiou's most central San Francisco store (the sixty-store chain started with a shop on Union Street in 1974) is at 152 Geary Street. Clothes are trendy and in the mid-price range. However, if you go to the Georgiou outlet (925 Bryant Street; 415/554-0150), you'll find last season's sports clothes, evening wear, and such at a fraction of the original retail price. Be sure to check out the $5 racks.

Among other outlets shopping experts recommend are:

The Six-Sixty Center
660 3rd Street
415/227-0464

Yerba Buena Square
899 Howard Street
415/543-1275

Designer's Co-op
625 3rd Street (near Brannan Street)
415/777-3570

Designer's Outlet
300 Brannan Street, no. 102
415/957-5978

Esprit Factory Outlet
499 Illinois Street
415/957-2500
(Most of the stock consists of standard Esprit designs.)

The North Face Factory Outlet
1325 Howard Street (near 9th Street)
415/626-6444

(Even discounted, the merchandise is expensive, but
   quality is excellent.)

Bridal Veil Outlet
124 Spear Street
415/777-9531
(Bridal accessories, from garters to head coverings, are
   here in abundance.

Gunne Sax Discount Outlet and Gunne Sax Fabric
   Outlet
35 Stanford Street
415/495-3326
(This is a huge warehouse operation with everything
   from christening gowns to prom dresses. Be on the
   lookout for damaged merchandise. The yardage outlet is particularly useful if you want to make an item
   such as a jacket or scarf to match a ready-made
   Gunne Sax garment.)

If you happen to be in town when the **Third Street
Warehouse** (2325 3rd Street) has a sale, be sure to be there
when the doors open—usually at 9 A.M. Among the shops found
here are House This (415/565-0662; napkin rings, drawer pulls,
teapots, chairs, garden tools, picture frames, and the like);
Forza (415/865-5456; wall sconces, bud vases, wind chimes,
and other decorative objects); City Limit (415/621-0131; art-
related gifts of the kind found in museum shops), and Summer
and the Hat Man (415/522-5555; hats, scarves, and handbags).
Most of the participants in these sales do not accept credit
cards, so bring along cash or checks with identification.

Terrific discounts are also a big draw at the **Fashion Center
Sample Sales** (699 8th Street; 415/864-1561) when some three
hundred booths offer sales reps' samples to the public. There's
a $3 admission charge to the sales, which are held five times a
year. To find out when they're held, phone the center or send a
postcard with your name and address to get on their mailing
list.

If you plan to devote serious money to your discount shopping spree, you'll probably save a great deal by hiring a professional discount shopper to show you around. Suzie Davis's "Hunting Bargains" (415/892-1088), offers five-hour shopping excursions for $32 per person. The tours are tailored to accommodate the interests of the participants—clothing, jewelry, accessories, housewares, furniture, shoes, and bridal gowns. Shoppers are picked up at their hotels and delivered back to them. The tours operate every day but Sunday, and reservations are required.

There are several reasons why hiring a professional can save you money. First of all, parking is often nonexistent around the various outlets, and it's sometimes impossible to navigate down the narrower streets clogged with parked delivery vehicles. Secondly, you'll waste a good deal of precious time trying to locate many of the businesses, especially those on side streets. For example, **Bill Lingle's Knitting Group of California** (2101 Bryant Street; 415/285-9999) produces high-fashion sweaters that sell at retail from $80 to $400. Made of cashmere, mohair, camel, alpaca, linen, or a blend of fibers, some of the sweaters are heavily discounted at the little shop in front of Lingle's manufacturing space. But if you didn't know about the outlet, you wouldn't realize there was one. Also, professional discount shoppers and their clients have access to warehouses, designer showrooms, and wholesale businesses not open to the public.

Designer Clothes

Like most desirable cities, San Francisco has attracted its share of designers. One of the most innovative, **Babette Pinsky** (28 South Park; 415/267-0280) produces clothes that are so reasonably priced that they are definitely bargains. Among them, her eighteen-piece line of micro-fiber pleated separates is washable, wrinkle-proof, and oh-so-stylish. The coordinated components, which are sold in some three

SOMETHING OLD

Every Sunday, beginning at 9A.M., **Pier 29**—a major ship-building facility in World War II—becomes San Francisco's largest indoor antiques and collectibles market. More than three hundred dealers are on hand to sell their wares, and since there's quite a dealer turnover, the selection of items for sale is ever changing. Admission is $2 at the door. Early-bird buyers can pay $10 for the privilege of getting in before the market opens to the general public. Pier 29 is on the Embarcadero a little more than a mile north of Market Street and can be reached from downtown by taking Bus nos. 30 or 90.

For vintage clothing, costumes, and recycled outfits, check out the 2000 to 2200 blocks on Fillmore Street. That's where you'll find the cast-offs of San Francisco's elite for sale. (Nattily dressed mayor Willie Brown donates his Brionis and Armanis to the **Victorian House Thrift Shop,** 2033 and 2318 Fillmore Street; 415/567-3149 and 415/923-3237).

---

hundred department stores and boutiques in North America, range in price from about $70 to $300.

Another terrific San Francisco designer is Beverley Siri, whose **Siri Boutique and Outlet** is at number 7 on the narrow Heron Street (415/431-8873), where parking is impossible. Siri's creations are known for their classically simple lines and richly colored fabrics. Prices for current models are at their regular retail prices (dresses, $160 to $300; long gowns, $370; and jackets, $350), but almost everything from past seasons—all of which are still very much in style—are marked down at least 50 percent. And remember that regular retail price is not necessarily what you will have to pay at boutiques and department stores, since they are under no obligation to charge specified prices.

Harper Greer (580 4th Street; 415/543-4066), a popular

mail-order company that specializes in women's clothes from size 14 to 26, has its only retail store in San Francisco. The clothing is moderately expensive (jackets cost from $89 to $350; dresses from $95 to 280; pants from $65 to $175), but far more attractive than most styles designed for larger women. By the way, there are often coupons for 10 percent off at Harper Greer in the *Bay City Guide*.

Specialty Shopping

Tarasco (Ghirardelli Square; 415/931-0567) is one of the newer shops in this charming shopping complex. Located on the Lower Plaza, it's the place to go for upscale Mexican arts and crafts—Oaxacan black clay pottery, Talavera tiles, pounded copper from Santa Clara del Cobre, silver bracelets from Taxco, ceramics from Guanajuato. Marionettes, marble chess sets, and masks; jewelry and hand-carved boxes to put it in; toys, leather goods, and clothing are among the other items on display.

Builders Booksource (Ghirardelli Square; 415/440-5773) is a must for anyone interested in home improvement. Manuals for builders, books on interior design, design-oriented software, coffee table books on architects and their works line the shelves. Whether you need advice on transforming a fixer-upper, designing a garden, or making fine furniture, you're sure to find it among the store's forty-two categories of books.

The ultimate gift of the counterculture friend who has everything can be found at **In-jean-ious Active** (432 Castro Street; 415/864-1434) in the form of an alternative 11½-inch generic doll. These modified Barbie dolls are created by Paul Hansen, who by day runs the computer lab at San Francisco's Academy of Art College.

Hansen used to call his creations by such names as Trailer Trash Barbie (her platinum hair is black at the roots and a cigarette dangles from her lips), but In-jean-ious was served with a cease-and-desist order for trademark infringement by

Mattel, so he's currently renaming his creations. The former Drag Queen Barbie is a Ken doll with blue eye shadow, a wig, and fancy gown. Carrie Barbie wears a prom dress drenched in fake blood. The dolls are in such demand that there's a waiting list, and the original $60 price tag will probably go higher.

At **Cool Doggy-o's** (488 Green Street at Grant Avenue; 415/788-COOL) you can buy tie-dye T-shirts and Guatemalan collars for Fido; batik pet beds, herbal flea remedies, natural shampoos, and Indonesian hand-painted bowls to put his home-baked dog biscuits in. The multitude of canine-themed items for sale include mirrors, clocks, and greeting cards.

I am usually not a fan of refrigerator magnets, but those at **Magnetz** (106 Powell Street; 415/772-9942) are especially clever. Animals that make the appropriate animal sounds and telephones that ring cost $9.99. Personalized license plates go for $3.99, and San Francisco scenes sell from $1.99 to $6.99. Elvis "dress-ups," with magnetized clothes to put on the "King," cost $19.99. There are Dilbert "dress-ups" too.

Bell'occhio (8 Brady Street; 415/864-4048) carries an extensive array of gorgeous antique and imported ribbons, trimmings, and specialty gift boxes. If you want to look at some knockout fabrics, go to **Agnes Bourne** (Showplace Design Center, 2 Henry Adams Street; 415/626-6883), where you'll see patterns by designers including Los Angeles–based Gregory Evans, who worked as a curator for David Hockney for twenty years.

Earthsakes, with two San Francisco locations (2076 Chestnut Street; 415/441-2896 and One Embarcadero Center; 415/956-4555), specializes in nontoxic or planet-friendly items such as golf tees made from cornstarch and clothing fashioned from organically grown cotton. In 1996, the stores distributed a coupon worth $5 off any purchase of $30 or more.

The **Hospitality House Shop and Gallery** in the Crocker Galleria (50 Post Street, Level 1; 415/398-7124) features art created by homeless men, women, and young people. The selection of items for sale varies, but quality is generally high and prices are reasonable.

At **TeaCourt** (1411 Powell Street; 415/788-6080) you can taste before you buy, $3 to $5 per selection). Actually, this can be a bargain if you're a connoisseur who's going to invest in a pound of TeaCourt's Chinese teas, since they range in price from $16 (Lichee Black) to $280 (Bi Luo Chun and Imperial Dragon Well) per pound. Even if you don't plan to buy, it may be worth $3 just to be able to tell the folks back home that in San Francisco you had a cup of Huang Mao Feng. And it costs nothing to step inside and look around this fascinating shop.

For a taste of San Francisco, stop in at **See's Candies** (the 846 Market Street store is just around the corner from the Powell Street cable car turnaround). There you can buy the chocolates that many Californians think are the best made anywhere. California Brittle, Scotchmallows, and assorted buttercreams; mint and caramel patties, plus about four dozen other kinds of chocolate confections make choosing favorites difficult, but the price is right at $10.30 a pound. You'll be offered a free sample when you make a purchase, and coupons for free See's candy bars are often available at the visitor center at nearby Hallidie Plaza.

If you're in the market for tutus or tap shoes, **San Francisco Dancewear** (659 Mission Street; 415/882-7087) advertises the "largest dancewear selection in California."

Ethnic Items

The City's ethnic pockets are great places for finding out-of-the-ordinary items. At Japan Center shops you can buy Japanese vegetable seeds to plant in your garden, tea-ceremony utensils, and books on a variety of Japanese crafts. From the 5200 to the 6400 block on Geary Street you'll find several Russian stores where books, crafts, and products from Russia are sold. And almost every shop along Grant Avenue in Chinatown is worth a quick browse.

Just Looking, Thanks

If you like **furniture shopping,** you'll adore the Jackson Square area. And people who love to look at food—plus gasp at the prices—won't want to miss the gourmet section on the top floor of **Neiman-Marcus** (corner of Stockton and Geary streets; 415/362-3900). Prices are astronomical for the freshly made galantines, pâtés, petit fours, and other items, but you'll find an occasional good buy in the condiments section.

Although most of the merchandise at **Saks Fifth Avenue** (384 Post Street at the corner of Post and Powell streets; 415/986-4300) is expensive, you can find bargains there, too, such as the five tubes of lipstick in currently fashionable shades that come in a mesh case ($18.50).

Museum Shopping

If I had to choose just one category of stores in which to spend my San Francisco shopping money, The City's museum shops would win hands down. First of all, the merchandise is both out of the ordinary and of high quality. Secondly, almost all of the articles for sale represent good value.

The outstanding designs of the goods for sale at the **San Francisco Museum of Modern Art (SFMOMA) Store** at 151 3rd Street (415/357-4035) makes for delightful but difficult choices. Ceramic bottle stoppers in the shape of buildings, hands, and clown hats ($19.50) by San Francisco artist Susan Eslick, 100 percent silk scarves by California designer Hiroko Kapp ($50 to $55), and earrings of beach glass and silver by San Francisco jewelry maker Amy Faust ($56 to $76; necklaces in the $300 range) are among the articles produced by leading California artists and artisans.

There's also an extensive array of jewelry, housewares, and wearable art inspired by the works of modern artists such as Pablo Picasso and Joan Miro, and some wonderfully creative four-inch-high figures made from old Mardi Gras costumes by New Orleans's homeless artists. The store includes an interactive children's section with imaginative games and toys in a wide price range.

The **M. H. de Young Memorial Museum Store** (Golden Gate Park; 415/750-3642) features—along with replicas of Rodin statues and Asian bronzes—reproductions of paintings which hang in the museum. Less expensive items include gift wrap incorporating designs by the likes of Henri Matisse and puzzles made from copies of works by Escher, Van Gogh, and Kandinsky. Although most of the books focus on fine art, you'll also find them on such subjects as kites, birdcages, Shaker textile art, and the history of underclothes.

Two of my favorite museums are at Fort Mason (Marina Boulevard and Buchanan Street): The **San Francisco Craft and Folk Art Museum's Shop** (Building A; 415/775-0990) and the Mexican Museum's **La Lienda** (Building D; 415/441-0445). At the former, you'll be able to buy everything from African wall hangings and Native American beaded necklaces to wooden flutes and ceramics from Latin America.

Crafts from all parts of Mexico are for sale at La Tienda. Especially appealing are the fanciful papier-mâché animals from the state of Oaxaca, tiles from Puebla, and naive ceramic figures from various regions of the country. The shop also carries a good selection of books on Latin American art.

Bestsellers at the **Exploratorium Store** (3601 Lyon Street; 415/561-0390 or 800/359-9899) include the amazing "Pinhead" interactive sculptures that preserve the three-dimensional shape of anything they touch. Other favorites are the owl pellet kits that contain the balls of fur, feathers, and bones that owls cough up after they swallow their prey—kids from 8 to 88 find them fascinating to dissect. Also among the 650 interactive works of science and art for sale in the shop is the "Exploratorium Snack Book," which shows how to build classroom versions of more than one hundred of the Exploratorium's interactive exhibits.

You'll find ships in bottles ($9 to $65) at the **National Maritime Museum Store** (2905 Hyde Street Pier;

415/775-2665). At the **California Academy of Science**'s three gift stores (Golden Gate Park; 415/750-7330), items for sale include everything from seeds for starting a rain forest ($5.95) to Neapolitan flavor freeze-dried ice cream that's a favorite with astronauts ($2.50). And don't miss the outstanding selection of dinosaurs, games, and toys for kids.

Best buys at the **Ansel Adams Center for Photography Store** (250 4th Street; 415/495-7242) are matted 8″-by-10″ reproductions of the photographer's works, at $7.50 each. For a dollar, you can strike your own bronze mint medal at the **Old Mint Museum Shop** (88 5th Street; 415/744-6830). At **Museo Italo Americano** (Laguna and Marina boulevards; 415/673-2200), Sicilian ceramics bear price tags ranging from $10 to $90, Venetian glass jewelry costs from $10 to $60, and the selection of Pinocchios includes some for $3.

If you're in the market for artistic items made from recycled materials, it's worth a trip across the bay to the **Oakland Museum of California**'s gift shop (1000 Oak Street, Oakland; 510/238-3401). Glass heart-shaped bottle corks come in blue, red, green, lavender, and pink ($16). Attractive candlesticks made from bicycle hubs and cogs cost $24 each. Roses fashioned out of misprinted Mexican tin have barbed wire stems ($12 each), and evening bags made from old kimonos ($42 to $64) are among other recycled items.

The Best of San Francisco's Souvenirs

Of course you can find tacky mementos of San Francisco all over town—three-for-ten-dollars T-shirts, music boxes topped with rickety orange bridges that play "I Left My Heart in You-Know-Where." Fortunately, it doesn't take much more effort to find souvenirs that won't look corny once you return home.

In the lower price range you'll find refrigerator magnets and Christmas ornaments shaped like San Francisco landmarks (see above). Replicas of Victorian houses come in a wide range of prices. Capsules that burst with displays of the

Golden Gate Bridge and other San Francisco symbols when submerged in water cost only about $1, and Chinese lanterns (prices vary) become permanent decorations in youngsters' bedrooms.

At **Photo Concessions and Event Photography Services** (Pier 39; 415/296-8639), you can have a commemorative photo taken with the Golden Gate Bridge as a backdrop ($14.95 for the first picture; $7.95 for additional prints).

"Fog Domes," available at the SFMOMA store ($29.95), work like the classic snow dome, except clouds of fog, rather than snowflakes, swirl around a miniature replica of the museum. Also at the museum's store, nickel-plated yo-yos bearing the SFMOMA logo cost $16.50, and a rubber-stamp kit of The City's landmarks, including three styles of Victorian houses, Mission Dolores, the Ferry Building, the Palace of Fine Arts, City Hall, SFMOMA, and the Golden Gate Bridge costs $49.95.

If you have the bucks and want to buy an authentic piece of San Francisco history, $1,599 will get you a steel headboard made from the original pedestrian handrail of the Golden Gate Bridge (Golden Gate Bridge Furniture Company, P.O. Box 420706, San Francisco 94142; 415/441-1101). Or you might consider six-inch slices of the railing, complete with brass identification plates and certificates of authenticity ($44 each from EdB Enterprises, 6116 Merced Avenue, no. 172, Oakland 94611; 510/881-4717). One slice makes a dandy paperweight; two, a pair of very sturdy bookends.

San Francisco parking meters cost from $150 to $300, and authentic cable car bells start at $700 (reproductions $70) at **The City Store** (Pier 39; 415/788-5322), where you'll also find bricks from Lombard Street laid in 1922 ($75 to $125, and not my idea of very useful objects), and five-foot-tall fire emergency call boxes ($400 to $1,000). Reproductions of a cable car stop sign ($29.95) and of a Haight or Ashbury street sign ($20 to $25) are among the less expensive items for sale.

For many of us, the best souvenirs of all may be books, with lots of pictures—especially those of San Francisco architecture. **Borders Books and Music,** conveniently located at 400 Post Street (415/399-1633), has one of The City's best selections. And a few blocks off the beaten tourist path, **William Stout Architectural Books** (804 Montgomery Street; 415/391-6757) bills itself as "The City's Finest Architecture Bookstore."

Wherever you plan to shop, spend some time before you set out checking the free weekly and monthly magazines for discount coupons. For example, in 1997 *Bay City Guide* had among its discount offers 10 percent off nonsale items at the National Park Store (Pier 39; 415/433-7331); Harley Davidson T-shirts (Dudley Perkins Co., 2595 Taylor; 415/776-7779); on any purchase at Empire Sports (607 Grant Avenue; 415/788-1715); and 20 percent off the lowest marked price on any item at the Esprit outlet (499 Illinois Street; 415/957-2550). Look for the coupons at Hallidie Plaza Visitor Center and in all the free weekly and monthly San Francisco guides. Though these coupons vary from season to season and year to year, every time I've been in town I have found discounts on everything from yarn and wearable art to hiking boots and Levis. You will, too—so don't forget to pack your shopping shoes.

CHAPTER

6

Neighborhoods and Ethnic Enclaves

Since its early days, San Francisco has been a collection of neighborhoods—some named after their locations, others for the national origins of their residents. Each one is a distinct entity, different from the others.

When you ask a San Francisco resident for the location of a particular place, as likely as not the answer will be the name of a neighborhood rather than an address. And to complicate matters, in some cases there are neighborhoods within neighborhoods. For example, Russian Hill, Telegraph Hill, and Fisherman's Wharf are considered neighborhoods, even though all of them are part of North Beach. To add a bit more confusion, a group of neighborhoods can be linked together by a description of their location—people who live in the Parkside, Sunset, and Richmond Districts, for instance, are all said to live "out in the avenues."

Although all of the neighborhoods may not interest you, several of the following undoubtedly will.

Union Square, bordered by Geary, Post, Powell, and Stockton streets, is considered the heart of The City's commercial district. Adjacent Maiden Lane—a two-block-long alley—and the other streets radiating off the square are lined with upscale restaurants and shops, punctuated by flower stalls splashing color on the street corners. The square itself is an urban oasis of green grass, palm trees, and flower beds, where toddlers delight in chasing the pigeons and an occasional sidewalk orator tries to convert passersby.

The centerpiece of the **Embarcadero** is the Ferry Building, which opened in 1896. It's still used as the terminal for commuter ferries to Larkspur, Sausalito, Tiburon, Alameda, Oakland, and Vallejo. Piers north of the Ferry Building are odd-numbered; those to the south, even. Over the years, as shipping out of the port of San Francisco has decreased, many of the piers along the Embarcadero have been converted to other uses, such as the Antiques Mall at Pier 29, and the neighborhood has become a fashionable area of high-rise condominiums and apartments, shops, and restaurants.

The **Financial District** extends from Montgomery Street east toward the Embarcadero. Ranked as one of the top financial centers in the United States, it's also the area where you'll find some of The City's best traditional restaurants (crowded at lunchtime but great for dinner; see chapter 3, Solving the Dining Dilemma). Most of the briefcase-carrying men and women you'll see in the Financial District's canyons are dressed for success in well-tailored suits and just-shined shoes.

In the days when the riches from California's Mother Lode gold and Nevada's Comstock Lode silver came pouring into San Francisco, **Nob** (short for Nabob) **Hill** became The City's high point as far as the newly made millionaires were concerned. The Big Four—Mark Hopkins, Leland Stanford, Charles Crocker, and Collis P. Huntington—built mansions on the hill, where they entertained at lavish parties.

To this day, Nob Hill remains a fairly grand place, crowned by Grace Cathedral, Huntington Park, a bevy of grand old hotels, and the Masonic Center, where many of The City's premier musical events take place. The cathedral, one of the most splendid in the United States, is best visited on a clear day when light shines through its magnificent stained glass windows. The Episcopal sanctuary is also the venue for concerts throughout the year. Huntington Park is the scene of several annual events and a great viewpoint.

The imposing **Civic Center** is bisected by Van Ness Avenue, San Francisco's widest street. Among its showplaces are Davies Symphony Hall, the War Memorial Opera House, the Civic Auditorium, and City Hall. The newest building in the complex is the San Francisco main library, which opened in 1996. One of the most outstanding public learning centers in the country and among the most technologically advanced in the world, the library contains over one million books and four-hundred electronic workstations. There's also a children's discovery center as well as special rooms housing collections of African-American, Chinese, Filipino-American, and gay and lesbian works.

Through much of the twentieth century, **SoMa**—the area south of Market Street—was one of The City's most severely blighted areas. Then, in the late 1980s, a transformation began taking place. The Moscone Center, San Francisco's main convention and exhibit facility, was built, followed by Yerba Buena Gardens, a visual and performing arts complex with its acres of public gardens, an outdoor performance area, and a memorial to Martin Luther King. The stellar attraction of this neighborhood is undoubtedly the new **San Francisco Museum of Modern Art** (SFMOMA), now the second largest modern art museum in the United States. SoMa is also home to dozens of discount outlets (see chapter 5, Shopping and Souvenir Specials).

South Beach is San Francisco's newest neighborhood. With the collapse of portions of the Embarcadero Freeway in the October 17, 1989, earthquake and the freeway's subsequent removal, the downtown waterfront district has been transformed from shabby to chic. Promenades and tidal stairs descend to water's edge. Palm trees shade sidewalk cafes, and renovated lofts and newly built condos have become some of the hottest real estate in town.

The **Marina,** developed on the site of the 1915 Panama-Pacific International Exposition, is a stroller's delight. It's a favorite with joggers, sun-worshipers, and kite-fliers, too. A grassy playground stretching along the bay west of Fisherman's Wharf, the area offers stupendous views of the Golden Gate Bridge on a clear day. Mediterranean-style homes and flats fronting Marina Boulevard are considered prime residential properties, and nearby Chestnut Street is the location of some of the city's trendiest boutiques and restaurants.

Pacific Heights is another one of San Francisco's prestige neighborhoods, where consulates rub shoulders with luxury condos. Manicured lawns and flower beds surround stately Victorians, ivy-covered mansions, and exclusive private schools. This is a great area for leisurely meandering on a fine day. The Broadway bluff between Webster and Lyon streets is one of the most gratifying streets for strolling. And don't miss the Sprekels Mansion (2080 Washington Street), the Whittier Mansion (2090 Jackson Street), and the Bourn Mansion (2550 Webster Street).

St. Francis Woods, a small pocket of luxury in the southwest part of The City, and **Seacliff,** which borders the Pacific Ocean between the Golden Gate Recreation Area and the Presidio, are two other posh places to live.

The **Castro,** with its steep streets and spruced-up Victorians—often painted in contemporary colors—is San Francisco's best-known gay neighborhood. Among the district's attractions are boutiques, bookstores, and bars; the 1922 Castro Theater (429 Castro Street) with its mighty Wurlitzer organ; trendy restaurants, and the Names Project memorializing AIDS victims (2362 Market Street). The largest of the community's annual events takes place each June, when the **Lesbian, Gay, Bisexual, Transgender Pride Celebration Parade** attracts about a half million participants and spectators.

The **Haight-Ashbury,** bastion of hippies during the Summer of Love, flower-power days of the 1960s, is still known for

THE SHOUTING WALLS OF SAN FRANCISCO

Since prehistoric times, man has felt compelled to record the dreams, fears, and realities of everyday life on the walls of his world. But nowhere in the United States have those universal subjects been chronicled so explosively as along the streets of San Francisco's **Mission District.**

An extensive area south of Market Street roughly bounded by Church Street on the west and U.S. Highway 101 on the east, the Mission used to be the home of the city's working-class Irish, Germans, and Italians. Then, in the 1930s and '40s, Hispanics began moving in. Now, Samoans, blacks, and Filipinos live there too, but it's the Latin culture which predominates, with most sidewalk conversations and shop signs in Spanish.

While many of the shops are of interest to tourists, especially the Mexican groceries with their freshly made tortillas, tamales, and bakery goods, the district's murals—more than two hundred of them—are what attract most visitors to the area. Painted on walls, fences, buildings, and garage doors, they range in subject matter from the historical to contemporary protests.

One of the first storyboards came into being in 1972, when four art students from the University of California at Davis— from Mexico, Venezuela, Puerto Rico, and Los Angeles— collaborated to cover a 67-by-12-foot wall on 24th Street. The largest single concentration of murals is along nearby Balmy Alley, where fences and garage doors have been decorated through the years with murals whose themes range from the suffering of Hispanic peoples to everyday clothes hanging on a line.

One of the most elaborate murals covers the two-story facade of the Leonard R. Flynn Elementary School on Precita Avenue. Just down the block, at number 348, is the **Precita Eyes Mural Art Center** (415/285-2287). On Saturday, at 1:30 P.M., the center sponsors walking tours of the murals. The walks are preceded by a slide show which explores the history of mural-making, from the cave of Lascaux to the murals painted at Coit Tower during the Great Depression. The slide show and tour (it's about eight blocks long and passes forty

murals) take about two hours and costs $3 for adults; $1 for
seniors and people under 18 years. For $30, there is also the
city wide "Mexican Bus" tour of San Francisco's murals on the
third Sunday of the month, and a Mexican Bus ride from
SFMOMA to the Mission District, followed by the walking
tour on the fourth Saturday ($15). Reservations are necessary
for the bus tours and can be made by phoning the center.

---

its creativity and diverse lifestyles. Shops where vintage
clothing, books, and records are sold predominate on Haight
Street. On adjacent byways are historic hippie sites, such as
710 Ashbury Street (once home to the Grateful Dead) and 112
Lyon Street, where Janis Joplin lived. Masonic, Piedmont, and
Delmar streets are among the district's most architecturally
interesting.

More than twelve thousand people of Japanese descent live
in **Japantown** (called J-Town by the locals). The heart of the
area is a five-acre commercial complex crowned by a five-
tiered pagoda symbolizing eternal peace. At the **Nichi Bei Kai
Cultural Center** (1759 Sutter Street; 415/921-1782) Japanese
tea ceremonies are held monthly. In keeping with another
tradition, people often place offerings of food and flowers on
the altar of the **Konko-Kyo Temple** (1909 Bush Street;
415/931-0453).

Though it's interesting on ordinary days, Japan Center
becomes even more so when it serves as the venue for annual
celebrations such as the April Cherry Blossom Festival, when
a group of musicians present a *taiko* drum concert. Artisans
demonstrate calligraphy and dollmaking. Three costumed
dancers wearing lion masks perform the traditional *shishi
mai* (lion dance). There's sumo wrestling and a colorful, two-
and-a-half-hour-long parade.

The **Fillmore,** between Japantown to the south and Pacific
Heights to the north, contains a number of cafes, restaurants,
and upscale shops, especially in the **Upper Fillmore.** Another

Fillmore attraction is the magnificent view of the bay and Alcatraz from Alta Plaza Park (Jackson and Steiner streets).

Cow Hollow, between Franklin and Steiner streets, was the center of San Francisco's dairy industry during the late 1800s. The first dairy was established there in 1861, and thirty others followed. It was also a communal washbasin, for it contained Laguna Pequena, a small lake that was one of the area's few sources of fresh water (some rich miners sent their laundry to Honolulu and China to be washed).

Tanneries, slaughterhouses, and sausage factories were established in the hollow, their offensive odors wafting on the air to the affluent Pacific Heights residents and businessmen. Tannery wastes fouled the water of Washerwoman's Lagoon. Eventually, the offending plants moved elsewhere. The board of health banished the cows in 1891, and Cow Hollow became an area of Victorian residences and modest stores.

In the 1950s, interior decorators had discovered the pre-earthquake buildings of Jackson Square and started a trend by turning that run-down warehouse district into a veritable showplace. By the end of the decade, entrepreneurs followed their lead and began converting Cow Hollow's gingerbread Victorians along Union Street into boutiques, coffeehouses, galleries, and restaurants. Now, there are about 250 of them along the street and its offshoots, and the district has become one of The City's most popular with shoppers. It's also a great sidewalk cafe area where you can enjoy some of the best caffe latte in town, along with some of the best people-watching.

The **Western Addition** is home to a thriving Japanese community as well as its African-American residents. And you can experience cultures from all around the world without leaving the **Richmond District.** Bordering Golden Gate Park on the north, the Richmond, along its Clement Street and Geary Boulevard shopping areas, offers Greek delis and kosher meat markets, Russian bakeries, and an Irish pub. Since an estimated 35 percent of The City's Chinese-Americans live in the district, Asian food markets, restaurants, and dim sum parlors are numerous and not so tourist-oriented (or expensive) as those in Chinatown.

There are other neighborhoods as well. The **Inner** and **Outer Sunset** districts are just south of Golden Gate Park and are primarily residential, with row houses, apartments, condos, and single-family detached homes, as are **Ingleside, Park Merced, Glen Park, West Portal, Excelsior,** and **Diamond Heights. Bayview, Potrero Hill,** and **Twin Peaks** are noted for their views. And there are a dozen more neighborhoods as well.

San Francisco's North Beach Still Speaks With Italian Accent

San Francisco's **North Beach** isn't what it used to be. Gone is the Black Cat, The City's first openly gay bar. And though the **City Lights Bookstore,** at 261 Columbus Avenue, is still presided over by poet Lawrence Ferlinghetti, it's not the same as it was in the glory days when Ferlinghetti, Jack Kerouac, Kenneth Rexroth, et al established the beatnik beachhead in North Beach.

Finnochio's female impersonators still preen and prance in the lavish reviews at 506 Broadway, but the International Settlement, going strong in the late 1940s with its sidewalk barkers and girlie shows, has been replaced by Asian grocery stores and shops selling Italian gelato.

Masses of Hong Kong Chinese have spilled over from adjacent Chinatown, and many of the area's post-1906-quake houses have been gentrified by yuppies who have discovered that North Beach is not only charming, it's also an easy walk downtown.

So it is significant that the community's Italian roots have remained, despite the fact that the North Beach branch of the Wells Fargo Bank now has Oriental characters next to the sign that says *Parliano Italiano,* and the New Pisa and Columbus Cafe's neighbor is a bakery where you can buy fortune cookies and Chinese noodles.

Even today, when young Italians with relatives in San Francisco immigrate to the United States, they'll settle in North Beach, working at Uncle Joe's butcher shop or perhaps opening a coffee shop or restaurant of their own.

Time was when North Beach really was a beach; when a finger of the bay extended far inland between Russian and Telegraph hills. As portions of the bay were filled in through the years it grew to the size it is today—bounded by Bay Street on the north, Pacific on the south, and encompassing the valley between the tops of Telegraph and Russian hills.

It was an area that early on started speaking with an Italian accent, as immigrants began to come in waves from the old country at about the time of the 1848 California gold rush. Though some of the later immigrants came from the south of Italy, by and large North Beach's roots were transplanted from the northern part of the country.

People from each area in Italy specialized in certain businesses. The produce district was run largely by immigrants from Genoa. Tortellini, ravioli, prosciutto, and other foodstuffs were sold by those from Tuscany. The son of an immigrant Genoese family in the produce business, Amadeo Peter Giannini, decided that the Italian community ought to have its own bank, so he rented a building at 1 Columbus Avenue and opened the Bank of Italy. Later renamed the Bank of America, his bank became the largest in the world.

To this day, and despite its changing face, North Beach retains its rituals. At the court behind the swimming pool on Mason Street, the old men still play *bocce* (a game which tests players' skill at rolling the ball so close it "kisses" a smaller ball called the *palina*). And they get together for nonstop card games at the Portofino on Columbus Avenue near Green Street.

Perhaps the most important rituals involve the preparation of traditional foods. In spite of the Asian influx, Italians continue to dominate the area's culinary sphere. It's a place of bistros and bakeries, restaurants, coffeehouses, and delicatessens—most of them with either a Mediterranean or old San Francisco ambience.

At **Panelli Brothers Delicatessen** (1419 Stockton Street; 415/421-2541), where they make their own prosciutto, you can buy six-inch-high sandwiches for about $2. Gelato sellers' flavors include spumone, melone, cioccolato, and pistacchio. In the basement of **Victoria Bakery and Pastry Company** (1362 Stockton Street; 415/781-2015), an old brick oven about the size of the average living room is fired with a torch at about four o'clock each morning. Italians from as far away as Reno, Sacramento, and Stockton come to the North Beach bakeries every time they're in San Francisco to buy shopping bags full of *panettone* (a slightly sweetened, dome-shaped bread with raisins and candied fruits), St. Honore (a custard cream cake served at celebrations), and biscotti (hard Italian cookies that taste best dunked in coffee).

Delicatessen clerks chat in Italian under canopies of salamis, cheeses, and bottles of wine in raffia baskets. You'll find great mounds of tripe and tubs full of Italian sausage, row upon row of tins filled with olive oil, plastic bags of dried mushrooms, huge gunnysacks of dried beans, dried chestnuts, and squash seeds, and boxes of dried cod. Pasta is as likely to be in bins as in packages, and in more shapes—big and little shells, bows, ribbons, wheels, and tubes of all sizes—and filled with cheese, meat, or chicken.

Saturday and Sunday nights there's mandolin music at the **Caffe Trieste** (610 Vallejo Street; 415/392-6739). The pastries at the **Bohemian Cigar Store** (566 Columbus Avenue; 415/362-0536)—a fifty-year-old coffeehouse known for its outstanding cappuccino—are homemade and worth a special trip to North Beach.

The names of North Beach restaurants—many of them among the city's finest—roll off the tongue like pages of an Italian phone book—Bucca Giovanni, Caesar's, Calzone's, Caffe Puccini, Gira Polli. As you might imagine, items on their menus run the gastronomic gamut, from fettucine Alfredo and tortellini alla panna to veal piccata, calamari fritti, and chicken parmigiana (see chapter 3, Solving the Dining Dilemma).

If you want to cook Italian when you get home, the special kitchen utensils you'll need are at places like **Biordi Art Imports** (412 Columbus Avenue; 415/392-8096) and **Figoni Hardware** (1351 Grant Avenue; 415/392-4765)—zucchini corers, tomato presses, cannoli tubes, different kinds of cheese graters from various parts of Italy, and Carrara marble mortars and pestles for macerating fresh basil.

On weekends when the weather is fine, find a bench in Washington Square so you can watch the action around Saints Peter and Paul Church. You'll have a ringside seat as bridal parties arrive for the elaborately festive weddings traditionally held there. The church is so popular, in fact, that dispensation to have Sunday weddings has been granted in order to accommodate the people who want to get married there. First Communion processions are another charming Sunday sight.

North Beach's big annual celebration centers around Columbus Day, when the Italian community commemorates the discovery of America with a marathon of activities—the Queen Isabella Pageant to choose the year's queen, a three-day *festa* at Fisherman's Wharf, and religious processions complete with members of religious societies, cassocked priests, and altar boys in their white surplices marching solemnly along the parade route and a statue of the virgin carried on high.

Other events include special masses, the blessing of the fleet at Fisherman's Wharf, the reenactment at Aquatic Park of the landing of Christopher Columbus, and the annual Columbus Day Parade.

To get to North Beach from downtown San Francisco, take the no. 30 Stockton bus or the Powell-Mason cable car line.

San Francisco's Chinatown:
A Treat for Early Risers

Every great place on earth, I'm convinced, has a time of day when it's more special than at any other. For San Francisco's **Chinatown,** the most magic moments come in early morning.

Certainly, there's after-dark enchantment when serpents twining the lamp standards come alive in the glow of the pagoda-shaded lights; when Duck à l'Orange and exotic night-club entertainment beckon. And then there's the afternoon excitement of shopping for ivory and kimonos and teak. But I still choose morning. For that is the time when Chinatown belongs to the some one hundred thousand people who live there.

Women in quilted jackets make their way through gossamer wisps of fog, shopping bags on their arms. With a patience inbred through centuries of civilization, they painstakingly inspect the vegetables piled high in wooden produce boxes outside shops with names like Canton Market and Lee Yuen. While choosing their daikon and bitter melon and fresh ginger, they chatter with friends in the cadences of Yunnan or Kwangsi province, then make their way down the streets and through narrow doorways to their flats above the shops.

The grocery shops used to be on Grant Avenue, Chinatown's principal thoroughfare. Now most of the them have moved one block west and are concentrated along Stockton Street between Pacific Avenue and Broadway. Inside the stores, huge plastic bags of dried mushrooms lean against one-hundred-pound sacks of rice. Plastic packets of dried fish snacks, rice crackers, and pickled fruits share the shelves with Heinz ketchup and Hamburger Helper.

In late summer, giant stacks of red and gold boxes containing the traditional mooncakes—with good things like pineapple, almonds, and papaya inside—add to the stores' exotic flavors.

There are fish shops along Stockton as well, with galvanized tubs of giant oysters, pompano, and wriggling blue crabs, and places like **New Maxim's Bakery** (1249 Stockton Street; 415/986-1660), its windows displaying an ancient plaster of paris wedding cake with swans holding the columns between each layer. Glazed ducklings hang in rows along the tops of butcher shop windows above winning lottery tickets and slabs of sweet and sour pork ribs. Newsstands add even more color, with their girlie magazines and comic books from Taiwan. At the **Mee Mee Bakery** (1328 Stockton Street; 415/362-3204), two women sit at Rube Goldberg machines in the rear producing fortune cookies.

The early morning's old men gather in clusters on street corners and in front of newspaper offices, reading copies of the day's news posted in the windows. In their uniforms of dark suit and white open-collared shirt, they glance up occasionally, shaking their heads at the westernized younger generation making their way to jobs downtown, and at the schoolchildren, running without any sense of Chinese dignity to the bus stop.

At Portsmouth Square, clusters of Chinese elders in traditional dress talk, their conversations punctuated every now and then by a bit of tai chi. The younger Chinese who congregate at St. Mary's Square two blocks away take their exercise more seriously and follow leaders as they perform the centuries-old movements. "The old ones come to the park so they can talk to people who speak their dialect," says a park employee. "They come every morning to find out who died during the night."

Regulars congregate at the **Eastern Bakery** on Grant Avenue (no. 392; 415/392-4497) for breakfast too, eating steamed buns, lotus bean cakes, or fried eggs. "Used to be, everyone who came in spoke Cantonese," says a middle-aged waitress, "but now since people started coming to Chinatown from all parts of China, you hear every kind of dialect."

Baskin Robbins, with all thirty-one flavors listed in Chinese characters, is also open for business.

Double-parked trucks disgorge their wares. A florist's delivery man lines the sidewalk in front of a new business with red foil-covered pots of split-leaf philodendron and chrysanthemums, beribboned in red with gold characters wishing the proprietor good luck. Smocked clerks place wicker baskets of miniature tea sets, paper parasols, and embroidered satin slippers outside a variety store. Next door, a jeweler meticulously arranges jade and gold pendants on black velvet in his window.

It's prime window shopping time—to look at the Chinese cooking utensils at the hardware store, tablecloths embroidered in the People's Republic of China, Chinese string organs called *erh hu*, cloissone thimbles, plastic kites, hand-crocheted sweaters, paper fans, and capsules that burst into the Golden Gate Bridge or a San Francisco cable car when submerged in water. You find treasures and trinkets that you miss in the afternoon crowds.

The most intriguing windows to westerners are the herbalists', with ceramic dishes containing age-old remedies like dried rattlesnakes (for warming up the cold blooded), newborn mice (for curing asthma), and fetus of barking deer, a teaspoon of which is recommended for clearing the throat.

Morning is a good time, too, for exploring Chinatown's alleyways—narrow passages that once were flanked by prostitution houses, gambling parlors, and opium dens. Ross Alley is one of the best for strolling, with its glimpses of women working at their sewing machines in garment factories and the sounds of clicking mah jong tiles.

Without the illuminated paper lanterns and evening's sightseeing throngs, Chinatown may lose some of its romantic appeal—but it gains the flavor one usually has to cross oceans to find.

* * *

While many San Francisco residents in such areas as the Sunset have lived in their homes for decades, other neighborhoods—especially those where newly arrived immigrants congregate—are ever changing, as successful residents move to more affluent neighborhoods.

CHAPTER
7
Sights Worth Seeing

Not only is San Francisco one of the most scenic cities in the world, it's one of the most compact. That means you'll have more exciting things to see per hour and spend less to see them—a real bargain for travelers who want maximum sightseeing at minimum cost.

Whether you set out with a detailed sight-seeing itinerary in mind or just walk out your hotel entrance and wander, San Francisco will show you amazing variety. You may choose to explore one of the neighborhoods or an ethnic enclave or concentrate on seeing as many of The City's Victorians as you can. Or perhaps you'll decide to follow a Bayside promenade one day and walk on the beach listening to the Pacific surf the next.

Among the sights you'll see are some of the most photogenic views in the world, open spaces more vast than in any other U.S. city its size, and architectural styles ranging from Victorian and art deco to classic and West Coast contemporary.

Open Spaces

San Francisco has more open space—in excess of 8,100 acres—than any city its size in the country. The best known oasis of green is **Golden Gate Park.** Stretching for more than three miles on The City's western edge, the park holds an assortment of wonders—both natural and man-made.

VIEWS FROM THE TOP

No doubt about it, on a clear day in San Francisco you may not be able to see forever, but you will have the greatest number of dazzling views in the United States. Some of them will best be seen from street level, others from The City's high points. Here are some suggestions on where to go. All but two of them are free.

• **Twin Peaks,** in the center of San Francisco, provides marvelous panoramic views. There's limited parking at the turnout, so try to get there before the tourist buses arrive.

• Look toward the bay from the Hyde Street cable car as it climbs to the top of Russian Hill for a terrific view of San Francisco Bay, Alcatraz, and Angel Island.

• It costs $4 (there's a $1 discount coupon available) to go up to the **SkyDeck** at Embarcadero Center (Market Street and the Embarcadero; 800/733-6318), but the 360-degree view is fabulous. It's open 5 to 10 P.M. Wednesday and Thursday; 10 A.M. to 10 P.M. weekends and holidays; closed Monday and Tuesday.

• Two large, breezy plazas on the seventh floor of One Market Plaza (Spear Street entrance between Market and Mission) provide panoramic bay views (use the elevators on the far right of the entrance).

• Board the no. 39 bus at Washington Square in North Beach and ride to **Coit Tower.** Take the elevator to the tower's 210-foot-high observation deck to watch ships coming into the harbor and a whole photo album full of scenes.

The east side of the park is where you'll find the museums (see chapter 8, Attractions and Entertainment) and the more formal botanical displays—the **Japanese Tea Garden, Strybing Arboretum,** and the **Conservatory of Flowers.**

Throughout the park, opportunities for exercise abound: a nine-hole golf course (415/751-8987; $10 greens fee on weekdays, $13 on weekends); twenty-one tennis courts

(415/753-7101; $4 for one and one-half hours on weekdays; $6 for a reserved court for one and one-half hours on weekends; $5 for walk-ons—reservations are suggested; people under eighteen are not charged for court use); and boating on **Stow Lake** from 9 A.M. to 4 P.M., Tuesday to Sunday, September through May. Riding lessons are given at **Golden Gate Park Stables** (John F. Kennedy Drive at 36th Avenue; 415/668-7360) at prices ranging from $15 to $30 an hour. There are baseball diamonds, polo grounds, croquet, lawn bowling greens, an archery field, and fly-casting pools.

The long-neglected extreme western end of the park is now being given a $5 million fix-up. In addition, the **Dutch Windmill** and the **Beach Chalet** have already been restored. The windmill, along with the Murphy Windmill, which is still in a dilapidated state, provided water for the park in its early days.

The Beach Chalet, a two-story building which looks out on Ocean Beach, was once one of The City's best known landmarks. Designed in 1925 by architect Willis Polk, the chalet's murals depict San Francisco in the 1930s, with picnicking families, a fisherman, and an old man feeding the pigeons in Union Square as well as other scenes of that era. The chalet also features tile mosaics and wood carvings. The second floor, with its stunning ocean views, houses the Beach Chalet Brewery and Restaurant.

Other projects in the West End's future are conversion of an old log dump into parkland, a new multiuse trail with a paved strip for biking and in-line skating, new picnic grounds, an additional soccer field, and construction of a community pavilion.

The largest urban national park in the world, **Golden Gate National Recreation Area** (GGNRA) was created in 1972 as part of the movement to bring the national park experience to people who live in cities. Also encompassing sites in Marin and San Mateo counties, San Francisco's 4,800 acres of parklands wrap around The City's northern and western edges.

These parklands contain ships that conducted trade and carried immigrants, fortifications built to defend the harbor, and early recreation venues. Among the man-made attractions located on GGNRA lands are **Alcatraz,** the **Cliff House, Sutro Bath** ruins, the **San Francisco Maritime Museum,** and **Fort Mason Center** (see chapter 8, Attractions and Entertainment). There are stretches of beach, hiking trails, and jogging paths; playing fields and fishing piers; areas where you can go sailboarding and even crabbing.

Among GGNRA's outdoor pleasures, **Aquatic Park** features spacious lawns, a sandy shoreline, and plenty of places to sit and watch the hardy souls who swim in the lagoon.

China and Baker beaches are favorite sunbathing spots (swimming is dangerous off most San Francisco beaches, however). A sandy four-mile stretch along **Ocean Beach** is great for jogging or walking, but dress warmly, as it's almost always windy with waves pounding the shore.

Farther south along the coast of **Fort Funston,** you can follow a loop trail with views of coastal scenery and watch the hang gliders who take off from the fort's high cliffs. Other hikers' favorites are the shoreline and hiking trails at **Land's End.**

The **Presidio,** another Golden Gate National Recreation Area point of interest, was established by the Spanish in 1776 and maintained successively as a military installation under Spanish, Mexican, and American flags until its closure in 1989. During the almost 150 years it was a U.S. Army post, the Presidio served as a refuge for 1906 earthquake victims, and in World War II trained Nisei (Japanese-American) soldiers at the Military Intelligence Service Language School. Today the area offers eleven miles of hiking trails and fourteen miles of bike routes. **Chrissy Field,** an army air base from 1919 to 1936, has become a world-renowned board-sailing area as well as a bird-watching venue.

Visitors can tour the Presidio; maps and a self-guiding Main Post Walk are available at no cost. Those who are environmentally conscious will be impressed by the biological diversity represented on the site, with eleven endangered plant species and ten different natural communities supporting a spectacular array of insects (including a rare wingless fly), birds, and other wildlife, as well as plants.

And that's not all. **Angel Island,** a military fort that processed early immigrants, and Alcatraz, the notorious federal prison, offer more opportunities for open-space exploration and are also under GGNRA's stewardship (see chapter 8, Attractions and Entertainment).

Through Downtown's Canyons and Along the Waterfront

Open spaces aren't only in The City's outlying areas. Downtown has its pockets of pastoral pleasure as well. Since they're popular spots with brown-baggers who work in the nearby office buildings, arrive before noon if you want to find a bench at lunchtime.

Planted on top of the Moscone Convention Center North (747 Howard Street; 415/974-4000), **Yerba Buena Gardens** is divided into three areas. The five-and-a-half-acre Esplanade, with twenty species of trees, brilliant flower beds, and a butterfly garden in its northwest corner, has lots of benches. The Sister Cities Garden contains a collection of flowering plants from San Francisco's thirteen sister cities around the world, among them the Australian bluebell creeper from Sydney and trailing lantana from Caracas, Venezuela. There's also a two-hundred-foot-wide reflecting pool and a curved wooden bench half the length of a city block. The East Garden, smaller and more secluded, features a three-tiered fountain.

At the **Crocker Galleria** shopping complex are two outdoor gardens—the Rooftop Garden and the slightly smaller Garden Terrace. Other rooftop gardens open to the public are the Sun Terrace on the fifteenth floor of the Crown Zellerbach building at 343 Sansome Street, as well as gardens on the fifth floor of the Bank of California at 400 California Street, and the second floor of the Delta Tower at 100 1st Street.

Justin Herman Plaza, located at the base of Market Street, is the venue for free jazz, blues, and rock concerts at lunchtime. Shade trees and an extensive sweep of lawn, plus a fountain spouting thirty-thousand gallons of water per minute, add to the park's appeal. Benches along palm-lined Herb Caen Way and in front of the Ferry Building are marvelous places from which to watch the tugboats, barges, and sailboats on the bay.

There are many other patches of green throughout The City—**Stern Grove,** where free concerts are held in summer months (see chapter 8, Attractions and Entertainment), golf courses, and neighborhood parks.

The Hills and Bridges of San Francisco

Maintenance foremen claim that hard-driving San Francisco cabbies burn out their brakes every 1,500 to 2,500 miles, and that may well be true. The six steepest hills in The City are Filbert between Leavenworth and Hyde streets and 22nd between Church and Vicksburg streets (both 31.5 percent gradient); Jones between Union and Filbert streets (29 percent), Duboce between Buena Vista and Alpine streets (27.9 percent); Jones between Green and Union streets, and Webster between Vallejo Street and Broadway (both 26 percent).

The San Francisco Bay, fed by sixteen rivers, is also crossed by five bridges. Recognized around the world as the symbol of San Francisco, the **Golden Gate Bridge** spans the strait leading to San Francisco Bay. It's anchored off the bay's shores on the San Francisco side to the south and the Marin Headlands to the north by twin 750-foot towers. Two cables more than seven thousand feet long and containing seventy thousand miles of wire stretch over the top of the towers and are rooted in concrete piers on shore. The internationally famous bridge is 1.7 miles long and painted its signature color of international orange.

An estimated 1,200 people have officially taken the 235-foot plunge off the bridge since it opened in 1937, but it's believed the number actually is higher since many suicides may have jumped undetected.

Though not so dramatic, the 8.4-mile San Francisco–Oakland Bridge, commonly known as the **Bay Bridge,** is the longest high-level bridge in the world. It's actually two different types of bridges—suspension on the west and cantilever on the east—connected by a tunnel through Yerba Buena Island. The bridge is the third busiest in the country, with an average count of more than two hundred fifty thousand vehicles each day.

To the north, the cantilever-truss Richmond–San Rafael bridge stretches 5.5 miles, joining the hills of Marin County with the upper East Bay. South of the Bay Bridge, the San Mateo–Hayward Bridge (6.8 miles) and the Dumbarton Bridge (1.2 miles) connect the lower East Bay with the San Francisco Peninsula.

Seeing It All

For first-time San Francisco visitors, commercial tours are usually money well spent, since they cover the area far more efficiently than you can on your own. They also eliminate the problems of frazzled nerves and the driver being so busy negotiating turns and traffic that he or she doesn't get to see much.

Several companies provide tours. The biggest of them, Gray Line, offers a three-and-a-half-hour "Deluxe City Tour" that costs $28 for adults and $14 for children 5 to 11 (discount coupons of $2 on the adult fare are available in the free entertainment guides).

The tour includes Civic Center and Mission Dolores drive-bys, a stop atop Twin Peaks for the panoramic views, a drive through Golden Gate Park with a stop at the Japanese Tea Garden, drives along the Pacific Ocean, down Presidio Avenue, and across the Golden Gate Bridge, with stops to watch the seals and to view San Francisco from Vista Point North. Most of the tours offered by Gray Line have commentary in German, Spanish, Italian, French, Japanese, and Korean, as well as English.

The rather unusual four-hour "Silver Screen Tours" explores movie locales from such films as *Vertigo, Mrs. Doubtfire,* and *The Joy Luck Club* ($24, adults; $21, seniors).

The ideal way to get a smorgasbord of San Francisco sights is by hiring a car and driver (Carey-Squire Limousine; 415/761-3000; about $45 an hour, three-hour minimum). This is actually not so expensive if you have four people sharing, since the cost amounts to about $5 more per person than the bus and van tours. Also, the tour can be tailored to your interests and you'll be able to see more sights per hour, especially if you get a knowledgeable driver like Tom Urbina, who was brought up in San Francisco and knows The City as only a native can.

For visitors who want to tour The City in their own cars or by renting one, the **49-Mile Scenic Drive** is marked by blue and white seagull signs. A free map detailing the drive, downtown San Francisco, Golden Gate Park, and major highways in the Bay Area is available at the visitor information center on the lower level of Hallidie Plaza.

San Francisco From the Bay

The sight of San Francisco from the water is unforgettable. When you don't have a friend with a sailboat, or enough money to charter a yacht, there are plenty of options left. One of them is to take a bay cruise. **Blue and Gold Fleet** (415/705-5444 for information; 415/705-5555 for reservations) offers an hour-and-a-quarter cruise that costs $16 for adults,

$12 for seniors and passengers 12 to 18 years, and $8 for children 5 to 11 ($2 discount coupons are easy to find). The sight-seeing boats go under the Golden Gate Bridge, past Angel Island and Alcatraz, and along the waterfront. Boats leave from Pier 39.

The one-hour cruise offered by the Red and White Fleet (415/546-2700 for information and reservations) covers much the same route but costs $26 per adult, with the same prices for other age groups as Blue and Gold ($3 discount tickets are available). Boats leave from piers 41 and 43½ at Fisherman's Wharf. Tickets for both companies' cruises are subject to a $2 per ticket service fee if they're ordered by phone.

There is, however, a less expensive way to get out on the bay and see its million-dollar views. During the early part of the twentieth century, the world's largest ferry fleet operated on San Francisco Bay. Fifty of the ferries—side-wheelers, stern-wheelers, and propeller-driven—carried fifty million passengers, plus horses, carts, and automobiles, a year.

The opening of the San Francisco–Oakland Bridge in 1936 and the Golden Gate Bridge in 1937 shifted commuter travel from boats to cars, but recent years have seen the return of ferry service. Now the boats do double duty, carrying both commuters and people who want to see the sights economically. And there's a bonus in the bargain. You can get off the ferry, spend a few hours looking around (see chapter 11, Day Trips and Excursions), then hop on another ferry for the trip back—something you definitely cannot do with bay cruise boats.

Two companies operate ferries between San Francisco and Sausalito. **Red and White Fleet** ferries leave from Pier 43½ five times a day (11 A.M. to 4:50 P.M. on weekdays; 10:40 A.M. to 5:50 P.M. weekends and holidays). Sausalito–San Francisco ferries leave from 11:50 A.M. to 8 P.M. weekdays and 11:15 A.M. to 6:25 P.M. weekends and holidays. The fare is $11 round-trip for adults and $5.50 for children 5 to 11.

Golden Gate ferries make nine round-trips on weekdays

GETTING THE RIGHT ANGLE

If photography is an important part of your sight-seeing pleasure, grab your camera bag—with lots of film—and head for any of the following:

• You've probably seen pictures taken from Alamo Square at Hayes and Steiner streets—Victorian houses stair-stepping down the hill with The City's skyscrapers as a backdrop. The area is one of eleven historic districts designated by the department of city planning.

• The gateway to Chinatown at Grant Avenue and Bush Street is difficult to photograph, since you usually get lots of pavement in the picture. Time your shots to coincide with eastbound cable cars coming downhill into the intersection and that problem is solved.

• You'll get your best shots of the Golden Gate Bridge (and a place to park your car) from Fort Point in the Presidio, Fort Mason, and the Marina Green.

• For spectacular wide-angle views of the San Francisco skyline, go to the west side of Yerba Buena–Treasure Island (between The City and Oakland via the Bay Bridge) or walk along the pedestrian walkway of the Golden Gate Bridge. Unless the water is unusually calm or you are shooting very fast film, taking pictures of the skyline from a tour boat or ferry is usually unsatisfactory.

• From the top of California Street on Nob Hill you'll get a fabulous view looking down toward the bay.

• Taking tight close-ups of your subjects—the flower stalls at Stockton and Geary streets, the Chinese markets on upper Stockton, dancers at any of The City's ethnic festivals—will usually give you the best results, especially on days with gloomy skies.

• For some after-dark fun with your camera and tripod, prowl around Pier 39 for photo ops. Between the shops and restaurants are several openings onto the bay. The nighttime view looking toward Coit Tower is impressive, too.

Just about anywhere, the best times to take pictures are usually in early morning and afternoon. However, in San

Francisco, with its frequent morning and evening fog, you'll probably do more middle-of-the-day shooting than usual. Don't let the fog keep you from snapping the shutter, however. Just adjust your film speed so that you will have the proper light.

(7:40 A.M. to 8 P.M. from San Francisco; 7:05 A.M. to 7:20 P.M. from Sausalito) and six trips on weekends and holidays (11:30 A.M. to 6:55 P.M. from San Francisco and 10:50 A.M. to 6:10 P.M. on weekends and holidays). The round-trip fare is $8.50 for adults, $6.40 for children 6 to 12, and $4.20 for seniors. Boats leave from the Ferry Building. The one-way trip takes thirty to thirty-five minutes, and free Muni transfers are included in the ticket prices.

Even less expensive on weekdays is the trip to Larkspur, a forty-five-minute ride on Red and White Fleet ferries that costs only $5 for adults, $2.50 for seniors, and $3.75 for children 6 to 12 (prices double on weekends). A pedestrian bridge links the Larkspur terminal with Larkspur Landing Shopping Center, a complex with more than fifty shops and restaurants. If you're not interested in shopping, take the boat back to The City on its return trip.

The Golden Gate ferry system also operates ferries from the San Francisco Ferry Building to Alameda and Oakland. The boats stop at both the Alameda terminal near the Alameda Naval Station and at Oakland's Jack London Square. The one-way trip takes twenty minutes to Alameda and thirty minutes to Oakland. Round-trip fares are $8 for adults, $5 for seniors, and $3 for children 5 to 12 years. All fares include AC (Alameda-Contra Costa County) Transit and Muni transfers.

Strolling the Sights

If you enjoy walking and have reasonably good stamina, it's quite possible to spend an entire holiday sight-seeing in San Francisco without relying at all on mechanized transportation. Among the commercial tours offered are Wok Wiz Chinatown Adventure Tours (415/355-9657). Led by cookbook author Shirley Fong-Torres, the tours are available daily at 10 A.M. and 1:30 P.M., and begin in the lobby of the Chinatown Holiday Inn. The cost is $25 per person, with dim sum lunch (reduced rates for children and seniors).

Helen's Grand Tour of Union Square, Chinatown, and North Beach (510/524-4544) begins at 9 A.M. Monday to Thursday, and lasts three and a half hours. Participants meet in the Westin St. Francis Hotel lobby under the clock. The tour costs $100 for two people, $120 for three, and $160 for four. Reservations are required.

About fourteen thousand Victorians—most of them well preserved—are located west of Van Ness Avenue in the Cow Hollow, Pacific Heights, and Alamo Square neighborhoods. Most ornate are those built in Queen Anne style with towers, turrets, and steep gabled roofs. Decorated with arches, spindles, and art glass windows, most of the Queen Annes were built between 1890 and the turn of the century.

Victorian Home Walk (415/252-9485) costs $20 per person, lasts approximately two and a half hours, and begins at 11 A.M. in the St. Francis Hotel lobby. The tour route passes more than two hundred Victorians, including the one where *Mrs. Doubtfire* was filmed. Participants also get to go inside a Queen Anne Victorian and take a scenic trolley bus ride that passes by points of interest including Union Street, Russian Hill, Chinatown, and North Beach. The tour costs $20 per person and lasts approximately two and a half hours.

Javawalk (1899 California Street, no. 9; 415/673-WALK) is a two-hour trek starting at Union Square and winding through Chinatown, Jackson Square, and North Beach. It focuses on The City's coffeehouses and its coffee history (both James Folger and the Hills brothers got their start in San Francisco. A stop frequently made on Javawalk is at Caffe Trieste (601 Vallejo), and another is at the Bohemian Cigar Store, where it's claimed that Francis Ford Coppola worked on the script for *The Godfather.*

"Cruisin' the Castro" (375 Lexington Street; 415/550-8110), led by Trevor Hailey, shows tour participants interesting shopping spots and architectural sights, like the Castro Theater and the Names Project Museum, original home of the AIDS memorial quilt. It also gives them insight into how and why San Francisco became the "Gay Mecca of the World." Ms. Hailey, a resident member of the gay community since 1972, is acknowledged to be one of the Bay Area's top tour guides. The $30 tour price includes brunch at the Castro's premier garden restaurant, Caffe Luna Piena.

During the Flower Power Haight-Ashbury Tours (520 Shrader Street, no. 1; 415/221-8442), guide Rachel Heller traces the area's history from its days as a Victorian resort, complete with roller coaster and bathing pools, to the 1960s, when it became the birthplace of the hippie counterculture. The two-hour tour costs $15 per person.

There are also San Francisco walking tours that won't cost you a cent. The city guides of the San Francisco Main Public Library (Civic Center; 415/557-4266) conduct free weekday and weekend tours that focus on local history, architecture, and culture. Walks explore various aspects of The City, such as ethnic neighborhoods, streets lined with Victorians, and out-of-the-way architectural treasures that most visitors miss. You can phone for a recorded schedule of the tours offered while you're in town.

To savor San Francisco's sights at whatever pace you choose, you might pick up the free "Pocket Guide to the Historic Districts of San Francisco" at the visitor information center and set out on your own. The guides includes a brief history of San Francisco and small maps of each of the nine areas that have been officially designated historic districts by the City and County of San Francisco, and tells about several landmarks in each district. Also included are illustrations and descriptions of the six building types featured in the guide, as well as numbers of the Muni bus or light-rail routes that serve each district.

You might also want to take a self-guided tour down gold rush–era streets and through Chinatown's alleys along the **Barbary Coast Trail,** San Francisco's official historic walking trail. The 3.8-mile route from the Old Mint to Aquatic Park is marked by 150 bronze plaques set flush into the sidewalks at every corner. It includes more than fifty historic sights and landmarks, including seven museums, several historic neighborhoods, and The City's three oldest public squares. You'll find the trail's description in a book called "Walking San Francisco on the Barbary Coast Trail," by Daniel Bacon, available for $13.95 at the visitor information center and at bookstores.

If you want to explore Chinatown on your own, consider renting an interactive audio guide ($12) from the Mark Reuben Gallery (334 Grant Avenue, 2nd floor, open between 8:30 A.M. and 6 P.M., or phone toll-free, 888/446-8687).

I usually prefer meandering to walking with a specific destination or purpose in mind. My favorite route begins at Union Square, then goes from Post Street to Grant Avenue, which leads to Washington Street, with Portsmouth Square on the right. Then I either angle my way over to Jackson Square and after that to Herb Caen Way along the Embarcadero, or I take Washington Street in the opposite direction to upper Stockton, with its Chinese markets, and proceed from there to North Beach (see chapter 6, Neighborhoods and Ethnic Enclaves). Plenty of resting places both at Embarcadero Center and Washington Square insure you'll be able to recoup your energy for the return trip. There's also public transportation nearby if you don't feel like walking back to your hotel.

It's also great fun to mosey around the Fisherman's Wharf–Aquatic Park–Fort Mason–Marina Green stretch, especially before all the other tourists arrive. Even when the crowds descend, however, you can always find a place to feast on the cracked crab and sourdough bread you've bought at the Wharf.

Russian Hill is another fascinating place to explore. Climbing the narrow stairways and walking along its streets will provide glimpses into a very special slice of San Francisco life. The hill, which gets its name from the Russian sailors who were buried in its soil, was once a haven for artists and writers, including Jack London and Mark Twain.

In addition to its brown-shingle houses, lush gardens, and bohemian charm, Russian Hill offers four historic districts and some of the finest views in The City—perhaps the most spectacular at the intersection of Vallejo and Jones streets. One of the historic districts is Macondray Lane, a path between Green and Taylor streets. Green Street between Jones and Leavenworth streets is another, with one of the two remaining octagon-style houses in San Francisco.

There's **Telegraph Hill,** too, which in the early days was topped by a semaphore signaling the arrival of ships into the harbor. Inside Coit Tower, murals created by twenty-six different artists depict life in California during the 1930s.

Though your leg muscles may not agree, the climb up the hill is worth the trip. For many years, Telegraph Hill was San Francisco's bohemia. Artists and writers rented cheap flats and hung out at the coffeehouses on the streets below. Today, it's one of The City's high-rent districts. (Whenever you're planning to do any hill climbing, bring a jacket because it can be shivery when the wind blows.)

Nob Hill is the place to go to admire the opulence of postearthquake San Francisco. In the nineteenth century, Crocker, Stanford, Hopkins, and Huntington, along with the railroad barons and bonanza barons James Flood and James G. Fair, built their homes on the hill and then filled them with the finest European furniture. Though the mansions built of wood perished in the fire that followed the 1906 quake, Flood's imposing 1886 brownstone at 1000 California Street survives. It's now the prestigious Pacific Union Club. Across from the club to the west is Huntington Park, where the centerpiece is a copy of Rome's Fountain of the Turtles, by Bernini.

Among Nob Hill hotels are the Fairmont (built in 1907) and Tower (completed in 1961). The Penthouse Suite at the Fairmont goes for $6,000 a night, with butler, maid, and limo service included. Through the years, another hotel, the Huntington, has been a favorite with royals and celebrities, among them the late Princess Grace of Monaco, Britain's Prince Charles, opera star Luciano Pavarotti, and movie star Lauren Bacall.

Most striking of the structures atop Nob Hill is Grace Cathedral, the largest gothic structure in the West. Completed in 1927, the cathedral's splendors include its Gates of Paradise doors, cast from those created by Lorenzo Ghiberti in the fifteenth century for the Baptistry in Florence.

Ten-Speed Sight-seeing

Although many areas in San Francisco aren't great for bicycling, those that are offer some of the most pleasant rides in the country. On Sunday, for example, John F. Kennedy Drive in Golden Gate Park is closed to vehicular traffic from dawn to dusk. The only hazards cyclists have to look out for are the bladers who share the road.

Any day of the week, bicyclists can ride from Aquatic Park along the shoreline to the Golden Gate Bridge. Crossing the one-and-a-half-mile bridge can be a real workout when winds are strong, but the great views of The City and the bay from the Marin County side of the bridge are worth the effort (ride along the bike lane parallel to U.S. Highway 101 to Alexander Avenue, which winds through Sausalito).

Pedaling through the Marina District, bicyclists get a close-hand look at art deco buildings, manicured lawns, and San Francisco living at its best. Just west of the Palace of Fine

Arts, (see chapter 8, Attractions and Entertainment), the Presidio offers a parklike setting for riders.

The flat, three-mile sidewalk along Ocean Beach, with its three bicycle lanes, can be combined with a ride around Lake Merced and nearby golf courses. Just ride south on the Great Highway two miles past the San Francisco Zoo to Sloat Boulevard, then turn right onto Lake Merced Boulevard.

Bicycle tours of the Mission District murals (415/285-2287) take place on the third Sunday of each month at 11 A.M. Cyclists with their bicycles and required helmets meet at the Precita Eyes Mural Arts Center (348 Precita Avenue). The tour costs $7 per person.

Wherever you go, remember to follow your instincts. If an area seems unsafe, it probably is. Carry your money—and not a lot of it—tucked away. That way you'll be able to enjoy the sights you see to the fullest.

CHAPTER
8

Attractions and Entertainment

Not only does San Francisco have outstanding restaurants, fascinating shops, and stupendous views, it also offers so many attractions, activities, and entertainments that it could take a lifetime of vacations to experience them all. Take the museums, for example. Because of a combination of wealthy residents with a philanthropic bent and the public's support of the arts, they're among the best in North America. The symphony, opera, and ballet are world-class, and the nightlife is dynamic.

Cataloguing the Museums

The **M.H. de Young Memorial Museum** (Golden Gate Park; 415/750-3600) is a traditional and impressive building containing twenty-two galleries of seventeenth- to twentieth-century American art. There are decorative arts, furniture, and sculpture on display, as well as paintings by Winslow Homer, James McNeill Whistler, John Singer Sargent, and other famous American painters. Many of the most important exhibits that come to San Francisco are shown at the de Young, including those that tour only three or four cities in the country. The museum is open Wednesday through Sunday, 10 A.M. to 4:45 P.M. Admission, also good for the Asian Art Museum, is $6, adults; $4, seniors; $3, ages 12 to 17. (By paying an additional dollar, you can visit the Palace of the Legion of Honor, too.) No admission is charged on the first Wednesday of the month, when hours are expanded to 10 A.M. to 8:45 P.M.

The **Asian Art Museum** (Tea Garden Drive, Golden Gate Park; 415/668-8921) displays ancient Chinese art treasures as well as contemporary Chinese masterworks. The largest museum in the Western world devoted exclusively to the arts of Asia, the museum's permanent collections represent more than forty Asian countries and span six thousand years of history.

This impressive array of art and artifacts from the Far East is further enhanced by a half-dozen or so major traveling exhibits each year, such as "Four Centuries of Fashion: Classical Kimono From the Kyoto National Museum," "Thirty Masterworks by Hong Kong's Greatest Contemporary Painter, Chao Shao-An," and "Splendors of Imperial China," an exhibit organized by the National Palace Museum in Taipei. Open Wednesday through Sunday, 10 A.M. to 5 P.M., admission is $5, adults; $3, seniors; $2, 12-to-17-year-olds. On the first Wednesday of the month (open 10 A.M. to 8:45 P.M.) and Saturday (10 A.M. to noon), no admission is charged. There is, however, an extra charge for major visiting exhibitions.

The **California Academy of Sciences** (Golden Gate Park) includes the Morrison Planetarium, the Natural History Museum, and Steinhart Aquarium. Admission, which includes the museum and aquarium, is $7, adults; $4, over 65 and ages 12 to 17; $1.50, ages 6 to 11. Admission is free on the first Wednesday of the month. There's an additional charge for planetarium shows.

The **Natural History Museum** consists of six halls devoted to: Wild California, Gems and Minerals, The Far Side of Science, Earth and Space, Africa, and Life Through Time. In the Earth and Space Hall, visitors are able to safely experience a simulated California earthquake. The Life Through Time—the

Age of the Dinosaurs Hall—demonstrates evolution as based on scientific evidence. The museum is open Tuesday through Friday, 12 to 4 P.M.; Saturday and Sunday, 10 A.M. to 4 P.M.

Steinhart Aquarium (Golden Gate Park; 415/750-7145) features the Fish Roundabout, a room surrounded by a circular one-hundred-thousand-gallon tank of ocean water filled with open-ocean fish. Smaller aquariums contain most of the Steinhart's collection of fourteen thousand marine creatures. The aquarium is open daily, 10 A.M. to 5 P.M., with expanded hours in summer.

The planetarium's five-thousand-pound star projector was specially built for its spot under the sixty-five-foot dome. Star shows are presented daily on the hour from 12 to 4 P.M., with additional shows on weekends, some holidays, Easter, and Christmas vacations. Admission to the shows is $2.50, adults; $1.25, over 65 and under 17. Laserium shows, presented Thursday through Sunday evenings, cost $6 for adults and $5 for people over 65 and from ages 6 to 12 (phone for program titles and times).

To reach the museums in Golden Gate Park, take a west-bound no. 5 Fulton bus on Market Street and get off at Fulton. After 6 P.M. and on Sunday's, take a no. 21 Hayes bus to Fulton and 6th Avenue.

The **California Palace of the Legion of Honor** (Lincoln Park, 34th Avenue and Clement Street; 415/750-3600 or 863-3330), which underwent a three-year, $34.6 million seismic upgrade and renovation in the early 1990s, is now one of The City's showplaces, with its older galleries enhanced and six new exhibition galleries surrounding a sky-lit courtyard, all part of an underground expansion. The museum's permanent collection is eclectic, with art from 2500 B.C. through the twentieth century. Open Tuesday through Sunday, 10 A.M. to 4:45 P.M. (the first Saturday of the month to 8:45 P.M.). Admission is $7, adults; $5, seniors 65 and over; $4, children 12 to 17. Entrance fees are waived on the second Wednesday of each month.

For five days each March, one of San Francisco's art museums becomes an indoor flower show. Bunches of tulips, daffodils, roses, and more exotic flowers are made into arrangements and placed throughout the featured museum's galleries by Bay Area florists and horticulturists. Many of the floral arrangements are designed to complement the colors and themes of the paintings, sculpture, and other works nearby. The museums' regular admissions are charged when they host this event.

When renowned West Coast architect Bernard Maybeck designed the **San Francisco Palace of Fine Arts,** the building was meant to be a temporary structure, lasting for only the ten months of the Panama Pacific Exposition of 1915. But San Franciscans fell in love with the Greco-Roman palace's sixty-six-foot columns and grand rotunda, so when the exposition closed, some thirty-three thousand of them signed a petition urging that the building be preserved.

Through the years, it has served as an art museum, a tennis center, a World War II motor pool, and a garage for diplomatic limousines during the days when The City was headquarters for the United Nations. Today it houses the **Exploratorium**— one of the finest museums of its kind in the United States (see chapter 10, Family Planning).

San Francisco Museum of Modern Art (SFMOMA; 151 3rd Street; 415/357-4000), designed by Swiss architect Mario Botta, is the second largest modern art museum in the United States. Among the major twentieth-century works on display are multimedia installations and photography, as well as sculpture and paintings. The museum is open Tuesday through Sunday, 11 A.M. to 6 P.M. and on Thursday evenings from 6 to 9. Admission is $7 for adults; $3.50 for students and people over 62; free for children under the age of 14. The museum is free to everyone on the first Tuesday of the month, and Thursday 6 to 9 P.M. admission is half price.

The **Cartoon Art Museum** (814 Mission Street; 415/CAR-TOON) became a reality in 1987 due to the efforts of a small group of cartoon art collectors and an endowment from cartoonist Charles M. Schulz. It is the only museum west of the Mississippi dedicated to the preservation, collection, and exhibition of cartoon art. Original drawings of newspaper comic strips and of comic book episodes, as well as original movie cartoon cels, are on display. There are pen and ink magazine cartoons, too. Temporary exhibits, such as one celebrating forty-five years of "Peanuts" comic strips, augment the eleven thousand pieces in the museum's permanent collection. Open Wednesday through Friday, 11 A.M. to 5 P.M.; Saturday, 10 A.M. to 5 P.M., and Sunday, 1 to 5 P.M. Admission is $4, adults; $3, students and seniors; $2, children. Informational sheets on the museum, found in the Hallidie Plaza Visitor Center rack, include a 50¢ discount coupon.

The **Ansel Adams Center for Photography** (250 4th Street; 415/495-7000) consists of five exhibition galleries. One of them is devoted to the photographic legacy of Adams, with many of his most important works on display. The other galleries contain contemporary photography as well as pictures by the master photographers of the past. Temporary exhibits have titles that range from "Japanese Landscapes" to "Posing for the Camera: Backdrops, Props, and Presentation," which covers everything from prephotographic imaging to computer-generated photographs. Open 11 A.M. to 5 P.M., Tuesday through Sunday; admission is $4, adults; $3, students, and $2, seniors and people 12 to 17. The Yerba Buena Center (see chapter 7, Sights Worth Seeing) is also in the same South of Market area as SFMOMA and Ansel Adams Center.

Another group of museums are on the bay at the north edge of The City at Fort Mason. By 1870, Fort Mason was a full garrison post with infantry and cavalry. During World War II and the Korean War, it was a port of embarkation for troops and supplies. Today, Liberty Ship *Jeremiah O'Brien* is docked at Pier 3 ($5, adults; $3, seniors; $2, children over 10; $1, children under 10 and members of the military in uniform), and a former Civil War–era barracks has become a youth hostel. The military warehouses are now utilized by more than fifty groups connected with museums, theaters, galleries, and various other forms of the arts.

The **Mexican Museum** (Building D, 1st floor; 415/441-0445) features works by Mexican and Mexican-American artists. Included in the museum's displays are preconquest, colonial, and folk pieces. The gift shop, which contains folk art from the different regions of Mexico, is itself a museum of sorts. Open Wednesday through Sunday, noon to 5 P.M., admission is $3, adults; $2, people over 64 and students with ID.

The **Museo Italo Americano** (Building C, 1st floor; 415/673-2200) is dedicated to researching, collecting, and displaying the works of Italian and Italian-American artists as well as promoting the appreciation of Italian art and culture. Museum hours are Wednesday through Sunday, 12 to 5 P.M., and admission is $2 for adults; $1 for people over 65 and students with ID.

The **San Francisco Craft and Folk Art Museum** (Building A North, Fort Mason; 415/775-0990) features an array of exhibits that go from the witty and elegant to traditional ethnic art and homespun crafts. Exhibitions range from "Have Birdcage, Hat Box and Silk Case; Will Travel" and "The Circus Collages of C.T. McClusky" to those showcasing arts and crafts of a particular country. Open Tuesday through Friday and Sunday, 11 A.M. to 5 P.M.; Saturday, 10 A.M. to 5 P.M., regular admission is $1 for adults, 50¢ for seniors and young people.

The **San Francisco African-American Historical and Cultural Society** (Building C, 1st floor; 415/441-0640) sponsors exhibitions and field trips to black historical sites. The first Wednesday of each month, from noon to 7:30 P.M., is Free Museum Day at the Fort Mason museums.

The **Museum of the City of San Francisco** (The Cannery, 2801 Leavenworth Street, 3rd floor; 415/928-0289) is full of interesting exhibits, from a recreated outdoor cooksite typical of those used by 1906 earthquake survivors to the three-and-a-half-foot head of the Goddess of Liberty from a statue that topped the dome of the old city hall: Vintage movie projectors—the Bay Area was the original home of the California motion picture industry—are also on display. Open year-round, 10 A.M. to 4 P.M., Wednesday through Sunday. Admission is free but donations are welcome.

Hello Gorgeous! (549A Castro Street; 415/864-2628), a combination museum and store, pays tribute to Barbra Streisand, with costumes, recreations of movie sets, and collectibles featuring Streisand. The downstairs store carries hard-to-find concert merchandise, music collections, and Streisand-related memorabilia.

Lyle Tuttle's Tattoo Museum and Shop (841 Columbus Avenue; 415/775-4991) celebrates one of the oldest arts known. It has been practiced in every country, culture, and social stratum from the time of the ancient Egyptians, and Tuttle's museum reflects the history, motifs, and mementos of the ancient art of body decoration. Classic Japanese designs of dragons and chrysanthemums, reminiscent of those painted on Oriental porcelains, are one of the displays. A book of sketches of tattoos made during the Boer War is another. There are brochures from the "King of Tattooists" George Burchett's parlors on Waterloo Road in London; a traveling circus banner advertising the legendary tattooed lady, Anna Howard; a display of World War II insignia, flags, and other patriotic symbols once popular with sailors. The museum is free and open during regular business hours.

The **Cable Car Museum, Powerhouse, and Car Barn** (1201 Mason; 415/474-1887) houses The City's first cable car (from 1873) and scale models of some fifty-seven types of cars which operated in San Francisco from 1873 to 1982, when the cars were put in mothballs. A gigantic fund-raising campaign, along with federal and state funding, rebuilt the motorless carriages' propulsion system and put them back in service by mid-1984.

Stabled in the barn are thirty-nine cable cars. Twenty-eight of them are "single-enders," which serve the two Powell Street routes, and eleven are "double-enders," which run along California Street. The former have one set of grips and are reversed on turntables. With grips both fore and aft, the double-enders can move in either direction and don't require turntables. The cars have a capacity of seventy or eighty passengers, but since San Franciscans have always looked upon their beloved cable cars as being elastic, they often carry more than the official capacity. The museum is open daily, November to March, 10 A.M. to 5 P.M., and April to October, 10 A.M. to 6 P.M. There's no admission charge.

At the **Old Firehouse,** which was San Francisco Fire Department Engine Company Thirty-three from 1896 to 1974 (117 Broad Street; 415/333-7077), you can sit in the driver's seat of a restored 1929 S.F.F.D. hook and ladder over fifty feet long. It's also free.

Commercial galleries are also museums of a sort, and since San Francisco embraces the avant-garde, it's especially interesting to go gallery browsing. At a recent showing, an installation featuring a twenty-foot-tall tower of Wonder Bread packages and an eight-foot-tall maze of cereal boxes was the principal work. Aluminum palm trees decorated with cerise styrofoam balls, wall hangings made from road trash, and giant bouquets of who-knows-what? are only a few of the artworks you may see.

This is not to say that traditional art forms are ignored. In fact, most of the galleries handle work by established local artists, and originals, prints, and sculpture by international artists. You'll find the greatest concentrations in the Union Square area along Sutter, Post, Geary, and Bush streets.

Across the bay, the **Oklahoma Museum of California** (10th and Oak streets; 510/834-2413) focuses on the ecology, history, and art of California. Open Wednesday to Saturday, 10 A.M. to 5 P.M.; and Sunday 12 to 7 P.M.; admission is $5, adults; $3, over 65 and those from 6 to 18. There's no admission charge on Sunday, 4 to 7 P.M. The nearest BART station, Lake Merritt, is one block away. The University of California campus, to the north in Berkeley, hosts a variety of arts-related events.

Optional Activities

Since food is such an important part of the San Francisco scene, it's only natural that cooking schools would be a part of it too. Unless you have plans to become a professional chef, you probably won't have the time to invest in a **California Culinary Academy** (625 Polk Street; 415/771-3536) course of study, but those who are seriously interested in cooking may want to take a short course or attend a demonstration at **Tante Marie's Cooking School** (271 Francisco Street; 415/788-6699).

Throughout the year, the school presents great chefs, such as Diana Kennedy, Giuliano Bugialli, and Lydie Marshall in demonstrations which last two or three hours and cost from $40 to $65 per session. At one holiday buffet demonstration, pan-fried Asian dumplings, potato latkes with smoked sturgeon and golden caviar, jambonneaux of chicken with roasted red pepper wrap, crispy potato and wild mushroom gratin, and ginger stout cake with caramelized pears were the dishes presented. A French cooking demonstration featured green pea and snow-pea soup, fricassee of lobster on a bed of celery root, and Valrhona chocolate cake.

One-week courses (about $700) and weekend workshops (about $250) are also offered at various times. A popular one-week course focuses on Italian home cooking, and weekend workshop subjects include everything from "cooking and preserving the autumn harvest" to "all about roasting and grilling."

If cooking doesn't light your burners, maybe horticulture does. In that case, head for **Acres of Orchids** (Rod McLellan Company, 1450 El Camino Real, South San Francisco; 415/871-5655). It's literally a paradise of parasites, with tropical garden settings providing the backdrops for thousands of orchids and other exotic plants. Tours of the famous nursery—it has more than one million square feet of greenhouses—are offered daily between 10:30 A.M. and 1:30 P.M. The nursery is open 9 A.M. to 6 P.M. (For additional factory tours, see chapter 10, Family Planning.)

Sports fans won't have to resort to TV to get their entertainment, especially if it's baseball season. The National League San Francisco Giants play their home games at **3-Com Stadium,** on the southern edge of The City. Known for the breezes that kick up in the outfield, the park has never been a favorite with players or fans, and a new one will be built in a less hostile location at China Basin, according to plans.

Across the bay is the **Alameda County Coliseum Complex,** home of the American League Oakland A's and the current venue for San Francisco 49er games. The stadium is accessible by BART, a ride of about twenty minutes from downtown San Francisco. Weather on marginal days is usually more pleasant than at 3-Com, and on good days it's delightful.

Very Special Events

San Francisco has always reveled in its diversity, so it is no wonder that the array of annual events is eclectic to say the least. There's a World Pumpkin Weigh-Off, a Cable Car Bell-Ringing Championship, the San Francisco International Accordian Festival, and the Saint Stupid's Day Parade honoring the patron saint of civilizations and parking meters, plus maybe a couple of hundred more celebrations that take place every year.

Among the best known of the annual events, the **San Francisco Jazz Festival,** offers an unbeatable combination of world-class musicians performing in a variety of venues, from elegant Nob Hill showrooms and auditoriums to a picturesque jazz cruise on the bay.

With an annual attendance of about fifty thousand, it's the most widely acclaimed jazz festival in the United States.

Featuring concerts, intimate club shows, and free outdoor performances, the festival showcases jazz in all forms, from contemporary to traditional, with blues, boogie, and Dixieland as well.

An example is the festival's "Stride Piano Summit," which puts the music of Fats Waller and other famous stride pianists in the capable hands of the likes of Dick Hyman and Ralph Sutton, two of today's greatest traditional jazz pianists.

The George Shearing Quintet, Wynton Marsalis, Sunny Rollins, Max Roach, and Dee Dee Bridgewater are among other performers who have appeared at festivals in the past.

The **San Francisco International Film Festival** has been held since 1957 and has gained stature with each succeeding decade. If you like foreign films, arrange to be in San Francisco during the last week in April and first week of May. Films are presented at the Kabuki Theater (1881 Post Street), the Castro Theatre (429 Castro Street) in San Francisco, as well as the Pacific Film Archive (2625 Durant Avenue, Berkeley) and the Lark Theatre (549 Magnolia Avenue, Larkspur). Festival information can be obtained by calling 415/931-FILM.

Another cinematic celebration, the **San Francisco International Lesbian and Gay Film Festival,** showcases more than 350 film and video works that have been produced around the world.

A new event, the annual **Gardens Gallery Walk,** takes place in early September, when more than two dozen galleries and museums in the Yerba Buena Gardens neighborhood are open to the public from 4 to 7 P.M. There is no charge, except at the San Francisco Museum of Modern Art. Entertainers perform and refreshments are served, there are special art-related activities for children, as well as drawings for prizes. Other special events for people interested in art involve five hundred artists who grant public access to their studios.

Each year the **Grand National Rodeo, Horse, and Livestock Show** attracts the best bareback riders, calf ropers, and barrel racers in North America. On **San Francisco Music Day,** a variety of bands play everything from Sousa marches to rockabilly at venues downtown. In late July at Golden Gate Park, top comedians entertain at a four-hour free "funnybone" frenzy called Comedy Celebration Day. In the world's largest run, the **San Francisco Examiner Bay to Breakers Footrace,** seventy thousand costume-clad runners vie to see who is the fastest.

Ethnic Festivals

The biggest annual ethnic festival is **Chinese New Year.** The Chinese identify their years in a twelve-animal sequence (rat, ox, tiger, rabbit, dragon, serpent, horse, ram, monkey, rooster, dog, and boar) in accordance with a complicated system of chronology dating from 2637 B.C., dictated by the lunar calendar. As a result, the date of the festivities varies from year to year, but they usually begin in late January or early February.

For tourists the centerpiece of the celebration is the parade, which begins on Market Street at Steuart, turns north on Stockton, east on Post, and north on Kearny to Columbus. The twenty-two-block route is packed with people craning their necks to see the floats that showcase the animal of the year as well as other Chinese themes.

The Chinese lion, Sze-Tsu, performs the lion dance. The 150-foot Golden Dragon with glowing eyes weaves its way down the streets dispensing one thousand firecrackers to dispel evil spirits. Giant puppets representing the "Immortals" and fan dancers wearing Chinese folk garb add to the colorful, noisy spectacle.

Other free events during the Chinese New Year celebration include the Chinese New Year Flower Market, where San Francisco's Chinese purchase the flowers, sweets, and red money envelopes so important to the traditional holiday (Grant Avenue from Broadway to Jackson Street and Pacific

Avenue from Stockton to Kearny streets). There's also a Chinese Community Street Fair with more than one hundred booths (Grant Avenue from Broadway to Washington Street, Pacific Avenue from Stockton to Kearny Streets, and Jackon Street from Stockton to Grant Avenue). At both these affairs there's lots of entertainment—Chinese opera, costumed dancers, martial arts competitions, and crafts demonstrations.

In March, the **Irish** have a turn to strut their stuff. In addition to the traditional St. Patrick's Day Parade, there's an Irish mass at St. Patrick's Cathedral (756 Mission Street) and a free St. Patrick's Day Block Party immediately after the parade at the Embarcadero Center, with entertainment by Irish dancers and musicians playing traditional Irish music. At night, a soccer game is played at Kezar Stadium between two of the oldest Irish soccer teams in San Francisco. Admission is $5.

Another free festival is the two-day **Carnaval** held during May in the Mission District. There's a big parade with huge puppets, steel bands, lavish floats, samba groups, and thousands of dancers and musicians costumed in feathers, sparkles, and spangles. What started in 1970 as a primarily Latino event has evolved into an international celebration with entertainment on two stages that includes groups playing everything from meringué and salsa to Afro-Cuban charanga, New Orleans zydeco, and rock.

In August, the **Filipino Pistahan Outdoor Fair** features a parade, a film and video festival, a folk-art exhibition, and an outdoor fair at the Center for the Arts, Yerba Buena Gardens. That same month, the three-day **Samoan Flag Day** celebration commemorates Samoa's annexation to the United States with traditional sports competitions, music, dancing, and ethnic foods.

Presented at the Russian Center (2450 Sutter Street; 415/921-7631), the **Russian Festival,** held in February, exemplifies the diversity of the Russian culture through crafts demonstrations, folk singing and dancing, regional foods, and cultural performances. The **Tet Festival,** held in the Tenderloin neighborhood, rings in the Vietnamese Lunar New Year in January or February. A month's worth of performances, exhibits, movies, and other presentations during February celebrates Black History Month.

There are other annual ethnic festivals as well—the Polish Spring Festival and Cinco de Mayo celebrations in May, the Festival de las Americas, Viva Mexico!, in September, October, and May. The Nihonmachi Street Fair, in August, and the April Cherry Blossom Festival take place in Japantown and at Japan Center. The Italian community celebrates in October at North Beach (see chapter 6, Neighborhoods and Ethnic Enclaves), and on June weekends the Ethnic Dance Festival (415/474-3914), with nine hundred dancers and musicians, showcases dances from around the world at the Palace of Fine Arts Theater.

The San Francisco Visitor Information Center maintains 24-hour telephone hot lines to provide information on everything that's going on in The City's entertainment world, from who's playing ball at 3-Com Park to who's singing the lead role in Aida. The information is available in English (415/391-2001), French (415/391-2003), German (415/391-2004), Japanese (415/391-2101), and Spanish (415/391-2122). There's also a Film Commission Hot Line (415/554-4004) that gives callers information on what movies and TV shows are currently being filmed.

It's Christmas in The City

You definitely won't hear the snow crunch, and you may not hear silver bells either, but there are so many compensations in San Francisco during the holidays that you won't even notice.

The season begins with a series of tree lightings and building illuminations. Pier 39, Ghirardelli Square, and Macy's are among the commercial establishments that light up trees of amazing heights while carolers sing and handbell choirs ring. Instead of a tree, the Grand Hyatt San Francisco extravaganza involves lighting the San Francisco Ballet's thirty-five-foot Nutcracker, while a host of Sugar Plum Fairies and other characters from the ballet dance around.

The five towers of Embarcadero Center and the Federal Reserve Bank building are outlined with more than seventeen thousand bulbs, and the San Francisco Museum of Art decorators string holiday lights around its signature turret.

Santas arrive by taxi and ferryboat. Some of them are seasoned pros, others come straight from graduation at the Western Staff Services Santa School (the graduation ceremonies are open to the public).

Holiday ice rinks are set up in Justin Herman Plaza at Embarcadero Center and in Union Square. Open daily from 10 A.M. to 10 P.M., a ninety-minute skating session costs $6 per person ($3 for children 8 and under) and the skate rental charge is $3 at Embarcadero Center, $2.50 at Union Square.

At Golden Gate Park, children 3 through 8 can ride horses through the woods to meet Santa ($12), and for children and adults, a Christmas ride through the park and a New Year's ride are offered as well (each costs $25 per participant, 915/668-7360).

At the San Francisco Maritime National Historical Park there are special holiday events, such as a sea shanty sing-along and storytelling aboard an historic ship at Hyde Street Pier. Admission to these events (dates vary each year) is $3 for adults; $1 for children 12 to 17). Children under 12 and seniors get in free. The park also hosts free "Christmas at Sea" parties aboard the S/V *Balclutha*. Reservations are required (415/929-0202).

It's in the sphere of theater, music, and dance that the San Francisco Christmas stars shine brightest. Each year from late November through the first week of December, the San Francisco Ballet presents Tchaikovsky's *Nutcracker* at the War Memorial Opera House.

Performances of Handel's *Messiah* are presented by a host of musical groups, including the San Francisco Symphony and Chorus and the Philharmonia Baroque Orchestra. If you want to do it yourself, several ensembles accompany sing-along *Messiahs,* and the Lesbian and Gay Band provide music for a dance-along *Nutcracker* (Center for the Arts Forum, 701 Mission Street; 415/978-ARTS). Playbills for the latter performance advertise that rental tutus and fairy wands are available for Sugar Plum wannabes.

"Beach Blanket Babylon," San Francisco's longest running musical review (Club Fugazi, 678 Green Street; 415/421-4222), has an annual holiday show that plays from before Thanksgiving until December 31, featuring tap-dancing Christmas trees and takeoffs on familiar carols.

Some of the season's most memorable musical events take place at Grace Cathedral on Nob Hill, where the natural acoustics and Gothic architecture add to the impact of whatever group is performing, be it the cathedral men's and boys' choir or a brass quintet. Prices start at $12 for general admission and go to $50 for reserved seating in the nave.

A number of holiday concerts are also presented at Old First Church (1751 Sacramento Street; 415/474-1608), ranging from Spanish renaissance airs to guitar duos playing music of the season. Tickets are generally $9 for adults; $7 for students and seniors.

There's an abundance of free musical entertainment, too, provided at various shopping centers. The Crocker Galleria, for example, sponsors concerts by the San Francisco City Chorus, the I Cantori Singers, the San Francisco Conservatory of Music String Quartet, and the San Francisco Opera.

Though the American Conservatory Theater does not present the holiday classic *A Christmas Carol* every year, when they do the production is first rate. Other seasonal favorites with children, such as *The Snow Queen, Hansel and Gretel,* and *The Velveteen Rabbit,* are also presented, but not always annually.

An event primarily attended by the locals, the Hamlin School's annual Holly Days gives tourists a chance to see this exclusive private school and enjoy its superb views of the bay while listening to live choral music and shopping at more than forty "boutiques." There's a children's fair, too. Admission to the early December event is about $4. (The school is located at 2120 Broadway between Webster and Buchanan streets; 415/775-4265).

For more shopping opportunities, check the newspapers to see what holiday crafts fairs are going on when you're in town. They're great as sources for handmade items, and you'll get the best bargains a couple of hours before closing, when stall keepers are thinking about all the goods they'll have to pack up and haul home.

At Calvin's Christmas-Garden Store (3525 Sacramento Street; 415/776-1280) you can buy San Francisco landmark ornaments of cable cars, the Palace of Fine Arts, Coit Tower, and the Ferry Building.

One of the most popular holiday events with San Francisco's Jewish population is Kung Pao Kosher Comedy Night, which combines Jewish jokesters and a Chinese dinner. Among entertainers who have performed are Sherry Glaser of Family Secrets and the Kinsey Sicks, a very funny gay comedy quartet. People start reserving table space in October, and tickets run out fast (415/431-7363 or 510/762-BASS).

On a more serious side, in Union Square menorah candles are lit each night of Hanukkah, and you can count on at least one Klezmer band performing traditional Yiddish and European folk songs somewhere in the Bay Area during the holidays.

Now, back to that snow. You will be able to play in it if you get to San Francisco early enough. In November at Pier 39, the Great San Francisco Snow Party is a skiing and snowboarding celebration with demonstrations, a learn-to-ski area, and a snow play area for the little ones. The snow is trucked in from the Sierras.

The-Price-Couldn't-Be-Lower Attractions

You can't go far in San Francisco without coming upon its street entertainers. They perform regularly, and present concerts at the Anchorage, the Cannery, Ghirardelli Square, Hallidie Plaza, Justin Herman Plaza at the Embarcadero Center, Pier 39, and Union Square. But you'll also see them in unexpected places: a saxophone player on a lonely corner in Chinatown; a tap dancer on Geary Street after theater performances; a brass quintet at one of the downtown BART stations. You'll see the very accomplished **San Francisco Mime Troup** (415/285-1717), too, at various locations in The City from July through Labor Day.

The **Stern Grove Midsummer Music Festival** (Stern Grove; 415/252-6252) provides a series of free 2 P.M. concerts on summer Sundays. The San Francisco Symphony, Preservation Hall Jazz Band, as well as other renowned music and dance groups perform in Stern Grove's verdant outdoor amphitheater.

The **San Francisco Shakespeare Festival** (415/666-2222), with performances on weekends from Labor Day through the first weekend in October, is free, too. Performances are presented in Liberty Tree Meadow behind the Conservatory of Flowers at Golden Gate Park. Also in Golden Gate Park, at Spreckels Temple of Music, free concerts are presented at 1 P.M. every Sunday from April to October. The Golden Gate organization is the oldest continuously operating municipal band in the United States.

When the Lights Go On

San Francisco is definitely not a city where they roll the sidewalks up. Whether you're looking for culture or conviviality, the ballet or a bacchanal, you'll be able to find it—probably in multiple choices.

The **Theater District** is located in the heart of The City, with eleven of the fourteen major theaters concentrated in seven contiguous blocks. Performance quality is high, and whereas in the past touring plays and musicals were the greatest financial successes, recent years have seen the increasing popularity of local theater companies, such as the **American Conservatory Theater** (ACT).

ACT performances take place in the recently renovated Geary Theater. Next door at the Curran, the productions are usually Broadway hits, often with their original casts. The Geary and Curran have been the Theater District's most important houses for more than fifty years, and their old-style grandeur adds to any evening's experience.

While most of the other theaters present mainstream works, the annual **San Francisco Fringe Festival** (415/673-3847) offers a marathon of provocative theater. On the festival playbill is a variety of noncensored comedy, drama, dance, and experimental works presented by international, national, and local performers. No play is longer than sixty minutes, and no ticket costs more than $7. The festival begins the first weekend after Labor Day and continues for ten days at five theaters within walking distance of Union Square.

In addition to the theaters downtown, others are scattered throughout The City. Works presented range from dramatic to musical comedy, one of which was the world premiere of a work called *Topographical Eden*, recently presented at the **Magic Theatre** (Building D, Fort Mason Center; 415/441-8822). The Magic's production was advertised with a blurb that read: "Will Honey at last find her mother in the Our Lady of Las Vegas Shrine in the Lady Luck Casino? Or will she be romantically distracted by the tattooed maiden riding her Harley into the sunset?" The Magic Theater, almost thirty years old, has developed and produced more than two hundred new plays, several of them by America's most important playwrights.

The **Lamplighter Music Theater** (Lundland Theatre, 175 Phelan; 415/227-0331) has been in existence for more than four decades, performing Gilbert and Sullivan operettas, and the **San Francisco Ballroom Dance Theatre** occasionally presents programs of tango, fox-trot, and other ballroom dances at Theater Artaud (450 Florida Street).

The **San Francisco Opera Company,** which moved back to the War Memorial Opera House for its seventy-fifth season in 1997 (the opera house underwent a multimillion-dollar face-lift, which included seismic renovations). One of the country's premiere operatic organizations, its thirteen-week season begins in September. In a typical season, nine or so works are presented, almost always including at least one each by Wagner, Puccini, and Verdi. The stage sets are marvelous and lead roles are sung by the top international stars, many of whom make their American debuts with the San Francisco Opera. Ticket prices range from $8 to $135.

The first Opera in the Park concert was presented in 1971, and since that time this has become the traditional final event of summer in the Bay Area. Nearly twenty-two thousand concertgoers attend the free program, held at Sharon Meadow in Golden Gate Park on a Sunday afternoon in early September. Stars from the San Francisco Opera's fall season perform arias from some of the world's favorite operas throughout the afternoon.

The **San Francisco Symphony** concert season features the world's top artists as guest soloists at almost all of its performances. Although top-price concert tickets cost as much as $70, the least expensive are often as low as $10. Also, now and then during the season, open rehearsals are held with an admission charge of $15.

In addition to regular performances by the symphony and guest artists, the Great Performances Series showcases groups such as the State Symphony of Russia and the St. Paul Chamber Orchestra. Ticket prices for these concerts vary, but usually start at between $12 and $23.

The **San Francisco Symphony Pops Concerts,** presented from mid-July through the first part of August at **Davies**

Symphony Hall (Van Ness Avenue and Grove Street; 415/431-5400) are less formal than those of its regular season.

The **San Francisco Ballet,** which performed at various venues while the opera house was undergoing renovation, is recognized as one of the top ballet organizations in the United States. Each year the company presents several world premieres and reprises of repertoire standards as well as new interpretations of classics (415/865-2000).

TIX Bay Area Union Square sells tickets for more than eighty performing arts organizations in the Bay Area, including the San Francisco Symphony, San Francisco Opera, and the American Conservatory Theater.

Half-price tickets are sold only on the day of the performance, except for Sunday and Monday performances, which are sold on Saturday. Show boards outside the TIX office list the tickets for sale that day. The half-price tickets are sold on a cash basis only, but full-price advance tickets can be obtained with Visa or MasterCard.

Open 11 A.M. to 6 P.M. Tuesday to Thursday; and 11 A.M. to 7 P.M. Friday and Saturday, TIX is located at 251 Stockton Street between Post and Geary.

When you're looking for less expensive entertainment, you can find that, too. During one week, the *San Francisco Examiner*'s Calendar listed free lectures on "The Genetic Diversity of Tomatoes," "Models for Understanding and Negotiating Religious Diversity," "Reasoning With Irrational People," "Court Sponsorship and Ideology in Ming Painting," and "The Songs of Johnny Mercer." Probably none of this is what you came to San Francisco to hear, but you never know when there will be a topic you've always wanted to learn about. There are free concerts, too.

You'll find that additional cultural events in Berkeley or Oakland are a BART ride away, and at venues in Marin County or on the Peninsula. To find out what's playing where, your best source is the Sunday *Examiner* Calendar section.

Checking Out the Clubs

My nightclub philosophy is this: If you're so inclined, you can sit in a bar and imbibe drinks made with the same ingredients just about anywhere in the world, so to get the most for your vacation nightlife money, you want to be entertained in a manner that's typical of the area you're visiting, with experiences different than you could have anyplace else. Most of the suggestions that follow are either San Francisco institutions or clubs, areas, or phenomena that are currently hot in The City. But it's a trendy town, so what's hot now may be just lukewarm next week.

Finocchio's (506 Broadway; 415/982-9388) features female impersonators in a cabaret show that has been a San Francisco entertainment staple since 1936. Costumes are lavish, and the impersonators, totally convincing. Admission is $14.50, and there are three seventy-five-minute shows nightly at 8:30, 10, and 11:30.

Not only has Finocchio's been around for a while, it's in an area that was San Francisco's first entertainment center. In the late 1800s, and at the turn of the century they called it the Barbary Coast. During the 1950s and '60s, jazz clubs and cabarets flourished in that same Broadway, Columbus, and upper Grant Avenue area of North Beach, with Miles Davis, Lou Rawls, and other greats appearing at clubs called Basin Street West, El Matador, and the Jazz Workshop.

By the mid-1970s, however, the area had become a derelict zone of sex shops and strip joints. But San Francisco has always been a city of phoenixes rising from ashes, so it's no surprise that North Beach's Broadway is coming to life as an entertainment mecca yet again.

The area is small enough that you can go club-cruising on foot. At **Moose's** (1652 Stockton Street; 415/989-7800) there's bebop and boogie one night, stride piano the next. At **Washington Square Bar and Grill** (1707 Powell Street;

415/982-8123), it may be a pianist and bassist playing swing standards. Both Moose's and the Washington Square Bar and Grill are restaurants where mature patrons as well as the younger crowd feel very much at home. Not so at the **Hi-Ball Lounge,** a very retro spot at 473 Broadway (415/397-9464), where a young crowd dances to live swing.

Waiters sing along with tapes of Italian pop stars at **Steps of Rome** (348 Columbus Avenue; 415/397-0435). **Frankie's Bohemian** is big and barny, with rock and roll reverberating to the rafters (443 Broadway; 415/788-0228). The dance club above Frankie's, Studio 435, is for those who want to relive the '70s disco scene.

San Francisco Brewing Company (155 Columbus Avenue; 415/434-3344) is housed in a lovingly restored 1907 Barbary Coast saloon. One of the first brew pubs in the United States, among its specialties are Alcatraz Stout, Gripman's Porter, and Emperor Norton Lager. Bargain time is from 4 to 6 P.M. and midnight to 1 A.M., when ten-ounce fresh microbrews cost $1 (pints are $1.75). Darts, chess, backgammon, cards, and dice cups, as well as a variety of musical instruments are available for patrons' amusement. On most evenings there's free live music, too, and tours of the microbrewery are available upon appointment.

Another area that's turned trendy is the Mission District. In fact, it's numero uno as far as Latino clubs are concerned. A clutch of clubs along the 3200 and 3300 blocks on 22nd Street include the **Lone Pine** (no. 3394; 415/648-0109), the **Latin American Club** (no. 3286; 415/647-2732), and **Esperpento Restaurant** (no. 3295; 415/282-8867). Those three, along with **La Rondalla Restaurant and Cantina** (901 Valencia Street; 415/647-7474) are among the more authentic hot spots in the Mission according to experts on the nightlife scene.

Slightly to the east, the SoMa is the third—and currently the hottest—in the trio of trendy nightclub neighborhoods. In the SoMa, **Kate O'Brien's Irish Bar and Grill** (579 Howard Street; 415/882-7240), is the place credited with starting the recent trend that's produced a bevy of Irish pubs, with one entrepreneur in the process of converting six existing bars into additional Irish watering holes.

There's also conjecture that a national trend may follow the San Francisco boom, which now includes Kate's, **O'Reilly's Irish Bar and Restaurant** (622 Green Street; 415/989-6222), **An Bodhran** (Haight and Scott streets; no phone), and the Irish Bank (10 Mark Lane; 415/788-7152), called the Bank of Ireland until the financial institution of the same name brought suit and won.

Though they may resemble traditional pubs, the newcomers have nights when ska, classic reggae, and northern soul are featured. Music on the juke boxes, however, remains strictly Irish, whether its recorded by U2, the Wolfe Tones, or groups playing ancient Celtic airs. At the club An Bodhran, on Sundays from 4 to 8 P.M., traditional Irish musicians of all ages sit in, playing a variety of music.

Another trend popular with Bay Area residents as well as tourists is **nightclub crawling by bus**. The tours—and I am not usually a tour fan—make a lot of sense. They are practical ways of sampling the nightlife without having to find parking places and wait in line to get into the clubs. Participants are able to drink without even thinking about driving, and since some of the clubs are in neighborhoods that can be dangerous, tours are safer than going on your own.

On the minus side, you don't have a choice in selecting other than choosing whether one tour's stops are better than another's. In addition, one club may turn you off even before the drinks arrive, while you would have been happy to spend the evening at another.

Of the nightlife tours available, Jazz Explosion (510/567-9721) participants get to visit four of The City's upscale jazz clubs. The $40 per person charge includes a beer or glass of wine at each club, cover charge, and transportation. Three Babes and a Bus tours ($30 per person) visit four clubs for thirty-five minutes each. The tour price pays for cover charges and transportation (with sing-alongs and other activities between stops), but not for drinks. Among the eighteen clubs that participate in the program are Babylon (2260 Van Ness Avenue; 415/567-1222), Johnny Love's (1500 Broadway; 415/931-8021), Julie's Supper Club (1123 Folsom Street; 415/861-0707), Frankie's Bohemian (443 Broadway; 415/788-0228), and Bahia Cabana (1600 Market Street; 415/626-3306).

Passengers on the Mexican Bus (415/546-3747) start the evening with a shot of tequila, south-of-the-border rhythms blaring from the bus's speakers, and a ride to the tour's first stop. It may be 330 Ritch (360 Ritch Street; 415/541-9574), Bahia Cabana Nightclub and Restaurant (1600 Market Street; 415/626-3306), or Sol y Luna Restaurante (475 Sacramento Street; 415/296-8191). Since new clubs come and go, become hot or not, the route of the Mexican Bus changes each weekend. The mix may include chic, new nightspots or hole-in-the-wall old-timers, but whatever the evening's chosen clubs, the music is sure to have a salsa, meringue, or other Latin American beat. The $30 per person cost includes cover charges and transportation.

With lesbians and gays making up an estimated 18 to 20 percent of San Francisco's registered voters, it's not surprising that the number of clubs with primarily lesbian or gay clientele is larger than in most other cities.

Rawhide II (280 7th Street; 415/621-1197) is The City's only full-time country and western bar. The clientele is primarily gay, but anyone who loves dancing can join in. Line and two-step lessons for beginners are given Monday through Thursday.

The **Stud** (399 9th Street; 415/252-7883) is a cutting-edge, gay dance club. "Tranny Shack," a regular Tuesday night event, features cross-dressed performance art and dancing to industrial rock. Featured attraction at the renovated and renamed **V/SA** (278 11th Street; 415/621-1530, formerly the Oasis) is a day-glo 3-D room with viewing glasses supplied.

Josie's Cabaret and Juice Joint (3583 16th Street; 415/861-7933) features a gay comedy open mike, and Tuesday is gay dance night at Bahia Cabana.

Views, Computers, and Lots of Laughs

You'll have to pay top prices when you have dinner on top-floor restaurants with **spectacular views** of San Francisco. You can have those smashing views without breaking the bank, however, by ordering a drink, soaking up the sights, and then going somewhere less expensive for dinner. Among the best after-dark aeries are the Carnelian Room (555 California; 415/433-7500), the highest man-made sky room from which to view The City; the Top of the Mark (Mark Hopkins Hotel, One Nob Hill; 415/372-3434), which offers a magnificent 360-degree view of the bay and the city (there's entertainment and a cover charge after 8:30 P.M.), and the View Lounge of the San Francisco Marriott (55 4th Street; 415/896-1600), with huge, seashell-shaped windows.

If your great evenings aren't complete without a computer, at **Cyberworld** (528 Folsom Street; 415/278-9669) you can surf the Web while sipping a latte or eating dinner. A membership card, good for six months, costs $2. Internet access is $4 for thirty minutes, $8 for an hour, and $2 for each additional thirty minutes, with a 10 percent discount for students. On Tuesday nights there's live music. On Wednesday nights you can access your e-mail for free.

Cobb's Comedy Club (The Cannery, 2801 Leavenworth; 415/928-4320) presents "name" comedians Tuesday through Sunday nights ($8 to $12, depending on the night and who is performing). On Monday night ($5) "Fourteen comics in a three-hour marathon" are the featured performers. Most San Francisco clubs cater to the 20s and 30s crowd. Johnny Love's, Babylon, and DNA (375 11th Street; 415/626-1409) are currently the favorite see-and-be-seen clubs. Your best chances of finding more mature crowds are at the jazz clubs, the lounges of the major hotels, and at the typically San Francisco shows like Finocchio's and "Beach Blanket Babylon."

The best source of information on who's appearing where is the Calendar section of the Sunday *San Francisco Examiner*. It lists live theater, symphony, opera, and ballet performances by groups throughout the Bay Area. Included in the section is a roundup of movie theaters in San Francisco and outlying areas, with information on show times.

9

Senior Savings Plans

San Francisco is Bargain City for seniors. Just about every-thing—from accommodations to attractions—carries a dis-counted price tag for those who have reached their sixty-second (in some cases their fifty-fifth, sixtieth, or sixty-fifth) birthdays.

If you fly to San Francisco, you may realize your first bargain when you buy your ticket. Each of the major airlines has two different **promotions** for seniors (usually for people 62 years and over). No matter which airline sponsors them, the programs are virtually the same.

One promotion offers books of four coupons, each of which can be used for a one-way ticket on the sponsoring airline and good for travel in the forty-eight contiguous states. Ostensibly, the coupons are valid for a twelve-month period. However, most airlines will allow travel to take place in the following year if the ticket is written during the first twelve months. In most cases, that means coupon book holders have two years in which to take two round-trips. As a general rule, the coupons must be converted to tickets fourteen days prior to departure, but standby travel is also permitted by some airlines.

Obviously, the coupon book savings vary, depending upon the participant's departure and arrival points. (Flights orig-inating at smaller airports such as Fargo, North Dakota, and Cedar Rapids, Iowa, usually involve greater savings than those from major metropolitan airports.) A big advantage of senior coupons is that they allow stays of longer than thirty days, since each coupon is good for purchase of a stand-alone one-way ticket rather than the round-trip tickets that often have length-of-stay restrictions. The 1997 price for most senior coupon books was $546.

The second promotion gives seniors a 10 percent discount on most tickets. Several of the airlines offer the same discount to the senior's traveling companion, regardless of his or her age. In addition, some airlines, such as Alaska Air, on occasion offer special senior discounts for midweek travel. There are times, however, when fares offered to the general public on selected routes are so low that no senior discounts are given on them. For seniors, these are often better buys than discounts offered especially to people in their age group.

Whether joining an airline travel club, such as United Airlines' Silver Wings Plus, is a money-saver depends on the travelers' destinations and frequency of travel. A life membership, which currently costs $225, gives the participant three $50 certificates, each good on United flights costing $300 or more during the two-year period from the first day of membership; a $100 discount certificate for travel to Europe; onboard credits from various cruise lines, and room-rate discounts at Hilton hotels and resorts in addition to special offers throughout the membership period.

Bed and Board

As far as accommodations are concerned, seniors can expect to get a 10 to 15 percent discount (and sometimes more) at most San Francisco hotels and motels. Some of these discounts require membership in the American Association of Retired Persons (AARP). Others are given to anyone who can show proof of eligible age.

The Kimpton Group, with fourteen hotels in San Francisco, regularly offers what they call Mature Traveler Packages and

Rates. At the various hotels, these rates ranged from $109 to $175.50, exclusive of tax, in 1997.

The "Young at Heart" package at the **Cartwright Hotel** (524 Sutter Street at Powell; 415/421-2865; rack rate $109 to $209), is available to guests 55 years or older or members of AARP.

It includes guest room accommodations, complimentary continental breakfast, afternoon tea service in the hotel's library, an evening wine reception, a complimentary workout at Body Kinetics, two California State Lottery tickets, and one complimentary in-room movie per stay. The package costs $119 per night in 1997.

At the **Harbor Court Hotel** (165 Steuart Street; 415/882-1300; rack rate $170 to $180, harbor view $180 to $190) on Friday, Saturday, and Sunday nights, the 1997 "Senior Saver" package for $125 included deluxe interior courtyard accommodations (bay view accommodations $165), use of the health facility and Olympic-size swimming pool, complimentary Pier 39 coupon book, two tickets to the Embarcadero Center SkyDeck, complimentary valet parking, and continental breakfast delivered to one's room.

You may find it to your economic advantage to join a hotel program for seniors, such as Hilton Senior HHoners. Designed for leisure travelers age 60 and over, the program (with a yearly membership fee of $55) offers room rates at up to 50 percent off at participating hotels. These rates are guaranteed to be lower than any of the hotel's publicly available rates with similar reservation and stay requirements.

The **San Francisco Hilton and Towers** (333 O'Farrell Street; 415/771-1400), had a regular double-room rate in May 1997 of $190 on weekdays and $170 on weekends, while the Senior HHonors' rate was $130. A 20 percent discount on meals in participating hotel restaurants, complimentary newspapers, and health club privileges, plus points toward hotel rewards and frequent flyer miles, are other program benefits. Since the San Francisco Hilton has a good deal of convention business and Senior HHonors rooms are subject

LEARNING WITH A SAN FRANCISCO FLAIR

For anyone 55 years of age or older who wants to give their San Francisco visit an educational twist, **Elderhostel** is a budget-oriented option. Spouses, regardless of age, are also eligible for the programs when they accompany an age-eligible participant.

In conjunction with the San Francisco Arts and Humanities Seminars, Elderhostel offers a variety of programs throughout the year. Headquartered at three sites and of either five or six days' duration, each program is based on a trio of subjects, with seven-and-a-half hours of class time devoted to each subject. Participants, expected to attend all classes on one of the three topics, may elect to attend all twenty-two-and-a-half hours of classes if they like.

Each of the programs includes at least one course that focuses on San Francisco, while accompanying topics explore everything from "Masterworks of Art: The Enlightenment" and "Hamlet—A Play for All Seasons" to "The Prison Industry in America" and "The Middle East: From Conflict to Conflict Resolution."

For example, topics for the May 11 to 16, 1997, session included "San Francisco's Back Roads," "Rococo to Romanticism," and "Get a Handel on Bach." Among the San Francisco-themed courses, "San Francisco's Unbeaten Paths" introduces participants to the history, architecture, and ethnic flavor of The City's diverse neighborhoods. "Popular Art in Public Places" explores the commercial sites and public squares which constitute San Francisco's outdoor museums. "San Francisco's Gold Rush Roots" studies the impact of the discovery of gold on the city by the Golden Gate.

Participants in the San Francisco Arts and Humanities–Pacific Heights programs are housed at the Holiday Lodge and Garden Hotel, a motor lodge with free parking (1901 Van Ness Avenue; 415/776-4469). Meals are served on the premises, and classes are held at the hotel's meeting room. A special lunch in the Careme Room of the nearby California Culinary Arts Institute is one of the program's highlights.

Headquarters for the San Francisco Arts and Humanities–

Union Square program is the Sheehan Hotel (620 Sutter Street; 415/775-6500). Formerly The City's main YWCA, this facility has been renovated and boasts the largest indoor swimming pool of any hotel in San Francisco. All meals are served at the hotel.

Participants in San Francisco Arts and Humanities–Post Street programs are housed in the Fitzgerald Hotel, a bed and breakfast in the heart of downtown (620 Post Street; 415/775-8100). Breakfast and lunch are served at the hotel, but Elderhostelers have their evening meal at the Sheehan Hotel.

Cost for the six-night programs, which includes lodging, all meals, and classes, is $415. The five-night program fee is $375. Additional savings are also available to participants. For instance, Grey Line city tours and tours of Sausalito and Muir Woods, regularly priced at $26, cost Elderhostelers $14. Tickets to certain performances at the Magic and Stagedoor theaters, Theater on the Square, and the American Conservatory Theater are available at 30 to 50 percent off. Admissions to museums and other attractions are also deeply discounted.

---

to availability, this discount has a much better chance of working for people whose trip dates are flexible.

Practical Packing

Bring in your hand luggage any medications you need to take regularly, and include copies of the prescriptions with other papers you carry on your person. If your medications require refrigeration, notify hotel personnel in advance so that you can have the use of a small refrigerator.

Whatever the season, you'll insure your comfort by packing an extra sweater. Summer mornings and evenings can get chilly when high morning fog blankets the area and more fog rolls in at night. A head covering will most likely come in handy, too. If you should happen to forget any pharmaceuticals or items that can be purchased at a drugstore, you'll get a

10 percent discount at the two **Wellman's Pharmacies** (1053 Stockton, 415/362-3622; and 728 Pacific, 415/788-8882) and at the seven **Merrill's Drug Centers.** (There's one at Market near 7th; 415/777-4550; and another at Sutter and Stockton; 415/434-4711.)

Travelers of all ages in need of medical attention while in The City can call **HotelDocs** (800/468-3537) or **Traveler Medical Group** (490 Post Street, Suite 225; 415/981-1102), both of which provide hotel room medical care.

Dining

Unfortunately, it's hard to find San Francisco restaurants that offer early-bird specials for seniors, or any other kind of dining discount, unless you patronize national chains like Denny's. And since part of dining is tasting regional flavors, you'll probably prefer eating at typically San Francisco restaurants.

One appetizing way of cutting down on dinner costs is to order two appetizers rather than an entrée, or an appetizer and soup rather than an entire meal. Another is patronizing ethnic restaurants serving small, less expensive dishes, such as tapas in Spanish restaurants and dim sum in Chinese eateries. San Francisco also has an abundance of delicatessens and cafeterias, which gives you the option of paying for smaller amounts of food than served to you in restaurants. Museum cafes also offer lighter fare at reasonable prices (see chapter 3, Solving the Dining Dilemma).

Attractive Attraction Savings

You'll find few bargains as far as sight-seeing tours are concerned. (Exceptions are some of the midweek ferryboat fares, which are especially attractive.) By contrast, almost every attraction in The City gives seniors a monetary break— one dollar here, half-price there.

There's one museum that's free to everyone and which will especially appeal to seniors. It's the Treasure Island Museum on the west side of Treasure Island, with a terrific view of San Francisco (415/395-5067). Site of the 1939 San Francisco World's Fair, it contains memorabilia from the late 1930s, including menus, sheet music, and lots of interesting photos.

10

Family Planning

San Francisco and kids are crazy about each other. The City provides more entertainment for children than almost any other metropolitan area. And whether they become enchanted with shopping in Chinatown, watching the boats at Fisherman's Wharf, or the exhibits at the Exploratorium, youngsters and teenagers will be in vacation heaven.

If you're flying to San Francisco, find out ahead of time what choices there are for children's meals. Though most airlines have kid-pleasers such as pizza, macaroni and cheese, or chicken nuggets and fries, you need to order them several hours in advance of takeoff time. Reserving airline space early will insure that you get those important window seats. Many airlines also give young passengers puzzles, games, coloring books, and other toys. For older children and teenagers, Walkmans with their favorite tapes work wonders to keep boredom at bay. And remember to pack bottles, "sippy cups," or pacifiers to ease little ones' inner ear pressure during takeoffs and landings.

Traveling by car, you might not get to San Francisco as fast, but you'll arrive in a happier frame of mind if you make stops along the way to let the children play or run around every few hours. And to sustain the happy mood, time your entrance to the Bay Area to avoid rush hour.

When you're packing, select clothes that the children usually wear during fall and winter—no matter what time of year you plan to visit San Francisco. Bring along warm jackets or coats for everyone. Hooded sweatshirts are handy, too, for boat rides and walks on the ocean beaches. Include one or two summer outfits if your trip will take place in September or you plan to make excursions inland.

Be sure to pack a few Band-Aids, children's aspirin, and sunblock (even though it's overcast you may need it on the water). Plastic cutlery and margarine tubs will save significant dollars if you plan to picnic frequently.

Whether you decide to stay in a downtown hotel or a motel away from the city center will depend largely on your family's interests and travel style, as well as the children's ages and temperaments. Though motels are generally less expensive than hotel rooms, there often isn't much price difference for comparable accommodations.

Children who need to let off steam frequently will probably be happier in a relaxed setting, with beaches and parks a block or two away. There are **parks and playgrounds** in all of The City's neighborhoods. Three of them near tourist areas are the Chinese Recreation Center (Washington and Mason streets), North Beach Playground (Lombard and Mason streets) and Huntington Park on Nob Hill, at California and Taylor.

With most youngsters, staying in hotels will be easier if there's plenty of action to watch from the windows or there are a lot of channels on the TV.

Very few hotels offer **family rates.** However, most of them allow at least one child in the adults' room, with or without an additional charge. You're more apt to find family rates offered by motels. For instance, **Vagabond Inns** (2500 Van Ness Avenue; 415/776-7500) offers a 15 percent discount with a coupon from the visitor center. That brings the regular rate ($99 for up to four people occupying the room) down to $84.15. Of course, in San Francisco, with its 12 percent room tax, a discount this size does little more than pay the tax. However, the special rate includes free continental breakfast, free parking (spaces are limited), free newspaper, and local calls.

Rack rates at the **Travelodge Hotel** at Fisherman's Wharf (250 Beach Street; 415/392-6700)—the closest hotel to Pier 39—are $135 to $185 in summer; $105 to $135 the rest of the year. Although the 15 percent senior discount is good anytime, the 10 percent AAA discount is in effect only during the slower periods, so if grandma and grandpa are along, let them register for all of you.

If you're able to get in on one of the special package rates at the **Clift** (see chapter 2, Bedtime Bargains), you can be sure your children will be treated like junior royalty. Items from baby bathtubs to balloons and baseball cards, electronic games and thermometers, can be obtained from housekeeping. There are books and board games available for use by young guests, too. At any time, guests traveling with children are allowed to book adjoining rooms at the single, rather than the double, rate.

At the less expensive **Hotel Beresford Arms** (710 Post Street; 415-673-2600), a jacuzzi junior suite costs $115, with no charge for children under 12. All suites include a choice of wet bar or a fully-equipped kitchen.

Mealtime can take a big bite out of family vacation budgets, but by planning a combination of picnics and meals at inexpensive, youngster-friendly restaurants, plus taking advantage of discount offers, you can eat well without spending megabucks.

At the **Hard Rock Cafe** (1699 Van Ness Avenue; 415/885-1699), if you belong to AAA, you can get a 10 percent discount on all food and beverages by showing your membership card before you place your order.

Chevy's (2 Embarcadero Center on Front Street, 415/391-2323; and 150 4th Street, 415/543-8060) is the place to take youngsters who like Mexican food. Staff members are friendly and have been known to give kids balls of tortilla dough to roll out at their tables.

At **Mel's Drive-In** (2165 Lombard Street, 415/921-3039; and 3355 Geary Boulevard, 415/387-2244), kids' meals come in boxes shaped like Mustangs, Chevys, and Corvettes. The Drive-Ins are '50s-style diners, with tabletop jukeboxes, vinyl booths, cherry cokes, hamburgers, and malts.

You'll probably want to feed the family sandwiches before you go to the **Toy Boat Dessert Cafe** (Clement and 5th Avenue; 415/751-7505) since peanut butter and chocolate cookie sandwiches and the like don't make for well-balanced meals. There are other treats in addition to those on the menu—a bucking horse in the middle of the room that children love to ride, as well as a large toy collection to look at.

Many of the attractions and activities highlighted in the attractions, sight-seeing, entertainment, and excursions chapters of this book will be enjoyed by youngsters, especially those of upper elementary school ages and older. A number of them charge reduced admissions for children under the age of 11 or 12; some also have special rates for teenagers. Still others offer family tickets.

The number one children's attraction is the **Exploratorium** (Palace of Fine Arts, 3601 Lyon Street; 415/563-7337). Inside the historic Greco-Roman structure is a huge, hangarlike area containing some seven hundred hands-on devices that explain every aspect of science. There are no paths or prescribed things visitors should do, for the philosophy of the museum is that staying within lines inhibits creative thinking. Therefore, kids and adults wander at will, watching the artists-in-residence constructing new displays, or learning about science and technology. Staff are quick to point out that "ideas," not traditional exhibits, are on display. When visitors have questions, they talk to an "explainer," who discusses the questions with them.

When it began in 1969, brainchild of the late Frank Oppenheimer (brother of famed physicist J. Robert Oppenheimer), the Exploratorium had a budget of less than $1 million a year. In 1995–96, that budget was about $14.5 million.

The increased funding and the guiding forces behind it have made the Exploratorium into one of the foremost discovery museums in the world. Areas are color-coded as to subject—weather, color, sound and hearing, waves and resonance, life sciences, motion, language, touch, patterns, vision, and light.

Within each area are displays like "The Turbulent Orb," which forms weather patterns like those found on Earth (kids can make mixtures of liquid soap and blue food coloring). At the "Bubble Window," children explore light reflection and refraction through a looking glass of huge bubbles. A "Distorted Room," an anti-gravity mirror, a tornado exhibit, lightning bolts flying from tesla coils—each device is intriguing, and scientific principles are reduced to their simplest form.

The Exploratorium is open Tuesday to Sunday, 10 A.M. to 5 P.M. (Wednesday 10 A.M. to 9:30 P.M.). It is also open Monday in summer. Admission is $9 for adults; $7 for seniors and students; $5 for people 6 to 17 and with disabilities, and $2.50 for children 3 to 5. Discount coupons are frequently available at the downtown visitor center, and admission's free on the first Wednesday of the month.

Another place that's "wonder-full" is the **Bay Area Discovery Museum** (557 East Fort Baker; 415/332-7674), located beneath the Golden Gate Bridge just south of Sausalito. Billed as "A Children's Museum for the Whole Family," and part of the Golden Gate National Recreation Area, the museum's hands-on exhibits involve crewing on the Discovery boat and crawling "beneath" the ocean. Exploring bridges, creating art projects, and making multi-rack sound recordings are among the other activities. Check to see whether art and photography workshops, hikes, or performances are on the museum's calendar while you're in town. Museum hours are Wednesday to Sunday, 10 A.M. to 5 P.M. (also Tuesday during the summer). Admission is $4 for adults and children over the age of one year. Discount cards are usually available at the visitor information center on the lower level of Hallidie Plaza. No admission fee is charged on the first Thursday of each month.

Not inexpensive, but probably an experience that falls into

the treasured memories of childhood category, is the Discovery Museum's "Gingerbread Architecture Studio" on December weekends. For $20 each, children get to make their own gingerbread houses to keep.

The only "floating" national park, **San Francisco Maritime Historical Park and Museum** (Hyde Street Pier; 415/556-3002), displays vessels both inside and out. Among them are the ferryboat *Eureka*, the steam tug *Hercules*, a coastal lumber schooner named the *C.A. Thayer*, and the paddle tug *Eppleton Hall*.

There's also the *Balclutha*, a three-masted, square-rigged vessel used for carrying coal, wine, and other goods between Europe and Cape Horn, and the schooner *Alma*. Admission to the museum, which includes entrance to the *Balclutha* and other vessels, is $3 for people 18 to 62 years and $1 for those between the ages of 11 and 17. All others are admitted free.

Also part of the S.F. Maritime Historical Park and Museum is the USS *Pampanito* at Pier 45, Fisherman's Wharf. A national landmark, the World War II submarine has been fully restored and gives visitors an insider's view of submarine life via a self-guided tour. During the year, park rangers present programs focusing on such subjects as steel ship construction and how steam engines make ships run. Admission is $5, adults; $3, children 6 to 12 and seniors.

The **San Francisco Zoo** (45th Avenue at Sloat Boulevard; 415/753-7080) is ranked as the sixth most important zoo in the United States. In a pleasant eucalyptus-shaded setting, it's the kind of place best enjoyed when you're not in a hurry and wearing enough clothes to be comfortably warm. Among its attractions are an African wart hog exhibit, a rare white alligator (viewable from late May through August), and the Primate Discovery Center, which features a nocturnal gallery. Koala Crossing looks like an Australian station in the outback, and there are islands where penguins and eagles dwell. Open daily, 10 A.M. to 5 P.M., admission is $7 for adults; $3.50 for people over 65 and between 12 and 17 years; $1.50 for ages

3 to 11. No entrance fee is charged the first Wednesday of each month.

Two free downtown museums with child appeal are the **International Children's Art Museum** (World Trade Center, Ferry Building, Suite 103; 415/772-9977; open Monday to Friday, 11 A.M. to 5 P.M.) and the **Wells Fargo History Museum** (420 Montgomery Street; 415/396-2619; open during business hours Monday to Friday), with its display of gold nuggets and a stagecoach that visitors can hop aboard.

The **Musée Mecanique** at the Cliff House (1090 Point Lobos; 415/386-1170), with 150 coin-operated machines on display, fascinates most youngsters. There are antique mechanical arcade machines, a toothpick carnival, and a variety of nickelodeons among the items exhibited. The museum is open daily, 11 A.M. to 7 P.M., and it's free.

A free story hour takes place on Tuesday and Thursday at 9 A.M. at **Charlotte's Web Children's Bookstore** (2278 Union Street; 415/441-4700), where $5 gift certificates are given to children who come in during their birthday month.

Free tours of the **Basic Brown Bear Factory** (444 De Haro Street; 800/554-1910) are conducted at 1 P.M. daily, with an additional tour at 11 A.M. Saturday. During the tour, participants learn how the bears are designed, cut, sewn, and stuffed. There is, however, a potential pitfall to taking the children on this tour. For a price, tour participants can select unstuffed bears of their own, help stuff them, then watch while an expert sews and grooms them. Then, after the newly stuffed toy is given a "bear bath," it's time to choose an outfit. Since bears cost from $14 to $150, and clothes from $3 to $16 per garment, this could prove to be a very expensive freebie. A great idea, though, for a child's birthday or special treat.

Another special treat might be a riding lesson at **Golden Gate Park Stables** (415/668-7360). One-hour group lessons cost $20, and pony rides are $4.

Also at Golden Gate Park, the children's playground, with its carousel, the buffalo paddock, and Spreckels Lake are attractions that will keep the youngsters happy. The lake is a favorite place for model tugboat, sailboat, and submarine owners to sail their craft.

For more shopping and browsing, if you can tell your children don't touch and they won't, bring them to **Kinder Toys** (1974 Union Street; 415/673-1780), where there are sailboats, playhouses, and all sorts of wonderful playthings to admire. A Kinder Toy postcard with tear-off strip good for a free poster is usually in the racks at the Hallidie Plaza Visitor Center.

You can rent in-line skates or traditional four-wheelers for skating on traffic-free John F. Kennedy Drive in the park on weekends and holidays. **Skates and Haight** (1818 Haight; 415/752-8375) and **Skate Pro Sports** (27th and Irving; 415/752-8776) are two shops where rentals, which cost about $5 an hour ($20 per day), are available.

On several days from June to September, Make*A*Circus visits San Francisco parks presenting free "Summer Festival Days." Each three-part festival starts with a professional theater show, followed by a free circus skills workshop, during which children can learn how to juggle, walk on stilts, and be a clown. In the third segment, the amateur clowns join regular company members in the circus ring to put on a show of their own (415/776-8470).

Very Special Events

Children's activities are often incorporated into festivals held throughout the year. For example, at the annual **Cherry Blossom Festival** at Japan Center, there's a children's village where youngsters can make arts and crafts projects, play games, race model cars, and watch puppet shows.

Other ethnic festivals feature dancing exhibitions and music that children as well as adults will enjoy. One of the best festivals as far as kids are concerned, however, involves people of all races and colors displaying creativity that ranges from

A SURE HIT WITH THE KIDS

One of the shopping places children and teenagers enjoy most is **Pier 39,** a honky-tonk, bayside boardwalk lined with shops and restaurants, outside eateries, and amusements such as "Underwater World" and "San Francisco: The Movie."

At the San Francisco Sock Market (415/392-7625), polka dots, hearts, flowers, and Scottie dogs—plus hundreds of other designs—decorate the stockings for sale.

One of the most entertaining shops is Wound About (415/986-8697), crammed floor to ceiling with windup toys. Dancing frogs and walking noses are among the more than two hundred items in the $1.99 to $9.99 price range. There are crawling cowboys ($14.99) and bears on unicycles. Helicopters, rocket launchers, and at Christmas, "Snoring Santas." Some pretty fancy fire trucks and airplanes cost $84.99, and windup pinball machines start at about $150.

Kite Flite (415/956-3181) is a blaze of color on even the foggiest day, with kites shaped like penguins, fish, and birds suspended from the ceiling. Kites cost from $10 to $400. At Swing Song (415/399-9504), the emphasis is on hammocks, wind chimes, and bells. Nutcrackers galore enchant browsers at Santa's Workshop (415/989-0353), and neckties for cats are a crowd-stopper at Kitty City (415/986-7684).

One of the newest attractions at Pier 39 is "UnderWater World" (415/623-5300), which takes visitors beneath bay waters inside a clear acrylic tunnel. Inches away, sharks, rays, salmon, jellyfish, crabs, and other residents of the San Francisco Estuary and Pacific Ocean swim unmindful of the humans peering at them. A thirty-minute narrated dive journey with headphones guides visitors along the moving walkways through the four-hundred-foot-long tunnel sixteen feet below the water's surface. Admission is $12.95 for adults; $9.95 for seniors; $6.50 for children 3 to 11 and the physically challenged.

If you want to patronize "UnderWater World," "Turbo Ride," or "San Francisco: The Movie" at Pier 39, be sure to get some "Cable Car Coupons" brochures at the Hallidie Plaza Visitor

Center before your visit. The brochure also contains coupons for the Medieval Dungeon, the Wax Museum, and Ripley's Believe It or Not, all along Jefferson Street at Fisherman's Wharf. These coupons are worth from 75¢ to $3.

Other coupons worth looking for are those that say "A Kid Eats Free" with the purchase of an adult entrée at the Alcatraz Cafe and Grill, and another that provides a complimentary bottle of wine with the purchase of an entrée at Dante's. Both restaurants are at Pier 39.

---

clever to bizarre. It's the **Street Performers Festival,** held in early June at Pier 39. Comedians, jugglers, unicyclists, slack rope walkers, and other entertainers provide nonstop entertainment. Even if you're not in town for the festival, you'll find street performers—some of them in outrageous costumes and strange-colored hair, some even with their bodies and clothes spray-painted—performing in the Hallidie Plaza area, at Fisherman's Wharf, Ghirardelli Square, and the Cannery, as well as in other parts of town on any weekend.

Each week in the "Kids" section of the Sunday *Examiner's* Calendar, more than half a dozen special programs—from Japanese toy-making demonstrations and magic shows to pumpkin festivals and poetry workshops—are scheduled.

Kiddie Culture

Several companies in San Francisco, including the Children's Theatre Association (Palace of the Legion of Honor, 34th Avenue at Clement Street; 415/387-7089), the New Conservatory Theater Center (25 Van Ness Avenue; 415/861-8972), ODC/San Francisco (700 Howard Street; 415/998-2787), and Young Performers Theatre (Building C, Fort Mason; 415/346-5550) present **plays and musicals** especially for children. Ticket prices are usually less expensive than those for adult theater.

Branch libraries throughout The City are a great source of

good free entertainment, presenting clown shows, story hours, and sing-alongs on various days of the week.

If a family outing takes you to Sacramento or the Wine Country, you'll want to stop at **Jelly Belly Candyland** (2400 North Watney Way, Fairfield; 800/522-3267) for one of the Herman Goelitz Candy Company's free factory tours. At the factory—their production capacity is forty million jelly beans a day—trail guides lead visitors along an elevated walkway above the production floor for a birds-eye view of state-of-the-art jawbreaker, jelly belly, and gummie making. The factory is the only place in the world where you can buy "belly flops"— jelly beans that don't meet company standards for size or color and are sold at reduced prices. To get to the factory, exit I-80 onto California Highway 12. Turn right at the first light onto Beck Avenue, then right on Courage Drive, and right again on North Watney Way.

When your destination is the Monterey Peninsula, you'll want to detour to **Santa Cruz,** with its **beach boardwalk and pier** (400 Beach Street; 408/426-7433). Centerpiece of the boardwalk is its 1911 Charles I. D. Looff carousel, a national historic landmark, which features two Roman chariots decorated with rams' heads and cherubs. The seventy-four carved wooden horses all have authentic horsehair tails. Best of all, it's one of only a few carousels in the world that boasts a working brass ring. Riders pull a ring when they pass the dispenser and try to toss it into the mouth of a giant canvas clown for a free ride. (Kids with good aim have been known to ride for hours.) Music comes from a restored 342-pipe Ruth Und Sohn band organ, one of the last of its kind in the world.

The old-fashioned boardwalk, even with some up-to-date attractions, such as the "Laser Tag Arena" and a trio of virtual reality experiences, evokes memories of the honky-tonk playlands of yesteryear. The roller-coaster ride is scary; the cotton candy sticky as ever, and the wide expanse of beach covered with sun worshipers.

While they're in Santa Cruz, teenagers won't want to miss

the **Santa Cruz Surfing Museum** (in the Mark Abbott Lighthouse on West Cliff Drive; 408/429-3429), where exhibits include surfboards, surfing attire (some of it fairly outrageous), and lots of photos. The boardwalk is open at 10 A.M. daily, Memorial Day through Labor Day, and on most weekends and holidays throughout the year it opens at 11 A.M. Closing times vary. Admission is free.

CHAPTER

11

Day Trips and Excursions: North

San Francisco's location, a little more than midway up the California coast, makes it a natural spot from which to take dozens of day trips and multi-day excursions. All of the destinations that follow can be visited in a day. Several of them, however, are well worth longer stays if you have the time.

Where you go should be influenced in part by the weather. Cold and torrential rain won't enhance the experience when you're exploring tide pools. And the Mother Lode in sizzling summer temperatures isn't much fun either. Therefore, we've included suggestions as to the times of year each place is at its best.

Most of these trips work best if you have a car. For others, you need to take only a ferryboat or bus. Commercial tours are available too, although not to all destinations. However, as we mentioned in chapter 7, it's possible to hire a car and driver for about $45 an hour.

When you want to rent a car but are leery of driving in downtown traffic, make arrangements to pick the car up at an agency that's away from the city center. Avis, Budget, Enterprise, Hertz, and Sears all have agencies in the Fisherman's Wharf area from which you should be able to drive relatively hassle-free to either the Golden Gate or Bay Bridge. If you're planning a trip south, picking up your rental car south of Market Street will allow you to avoid a good deal of the downtown traffic, or ride a bus to San Francisco International Airport and take possession of the car there.

Alcatraz, the notorious island prison, is one-and-a-quarter miles by ferry from Pier 41 at Fisherman's Wharf. Alcatraz began as a military fort in the mid-nineteenth century, became a full-time military prison in 1907, and served as a federal penitentiary from 1934 to 1964. Ranger walks, an introductory slide show presented in a theater near the dock, and programs highlighting military history, famous inmates, escapes, national history, and the Native American occupation are all free of charge. The subjects of each day's programs are posted, along with the presentations' locations. There's no charge for admission, but donations are welcome.

If you prefer to explore the prison and grounds at your own tempo, a free self-guided walking tour brochure is available. For the Alcatraz cell house tour, you might want to rent a cassette, which features narration by former correctional officers and inmates. Tapes are available at the cell house entrance for a nominal fee.

The island is eerier than usual on a drab or foggy day. Sunshine makes it more difficult to imagine what prison life was like. Except, of course, in the cell block where the clang of metal reverberates against the thick cement walls. And even if you visit on a sunny day, be sure to take along warm clothes, as wind blowing through the Golden Gate can chill you to the bone.

The ferry ride, including the use of a cell block audio cassette, costs $11 for adults, $9.20 for people 62 and over, and $5.75 for those 5 to 11 years. Without cassettes, the rates are $7.75, $6, and $4.50. Tickets must be purchased for a specific San Francisco departure time (boats leave at 9:30 A.M., 10:15 A.M., and every half hour after that until 2:15 P.M., but ticket holders can return from the island on any of the ferries that day. At certain times of the year, tickets must be purchased in advance, so make sure to call ahead.

Two thousand years ago, Angel Island provided good fishing and hunting for the Coastal Miwok Indians. Much later it was a cattle ranch, and after that a U.S. Army post. For decades until the 1940s, Angel Island was an immigration station for Asians as well as serving various military functions. Now extensively renovated, the island is part of the Golden Gate National Recreation Area. The Immigration Station Museum chronicles the history of the "Ellis Island of the West." There's also a one-hour tram tour with audio narration (departure from Cove Cafe next to the ferry landing; $9 for adults, $8 for seniors, $5 for children 5 to 12; 415/897-0715).

Thirteen miles of hiking trails along the island's ridges and beaches, and through its grasslands and forested slopes provide various degrees of challenge. Mountain bike rentals are available on a first-come, first-served basis ($9 an hour, $25 a day; child trailers, $5 an hour, $10 a day). Sea kayaking tours, which circumnavigate the island, focus on history and the environment. The six-hour tours, which include lunch, cost $100 per person.

Tours, bike rentals, and Cove Cafe, with its redwood deck overlooking the harbor, operate from mid-March through October. To get to the island, take a Red and White ferry from Pier 43½ at Fisherman's Wharf. Adult fare is $10; $9 for 12- to 18-year-olds, and $5.50 for children 5 to 11. Ferry prices include the park entry fee. There's limited bike space on the ferries, allotted on a first-come basis. Ferry service is available on weekends and holidays only, leaving San Francisco at 10:40 A.M., with boats returning at 12 and 4:50 P.M.

Sausalito, just across the Golden Gate from San Francisco, was once a whaling port and later became a bootlegger's haven during Prohibition. Since the 1970s, it has been known as an artsy, Mediterranean-style sort of a place that's great both for its views and shopping. You can find original art for sale at the Schoonmaker and Industrial Center buildings, where artists have their studios. The chamber of commerce (333 Caledonia Street; 415/331-7562) publishes a guide to the buildings which includes artists' on-site hours. There's a shuttle service from the ferry landing to the two buildings.

If you want information on the area, the Sausalito Visitor Center is on the fourth floor of the Village Fair building, at 777 Bridgeway; 415/332-0505.) To get to Sausalito, you can drive (the exit from Highway 101 is just north of the bridge), ride a ferry (see chapter 7, Sights Worth Seeing, for fares and schedules), or take bus line No. 10 or No. 50.

Less than a mile north of the Sausalito exit on U.S. Highway 101 is the exit to Tiburon and Belvedere—both good places to drive if you like to look at interesting architecture and landscaping. Although more than two-thirds of Tiburon's owner-occupied dwellings are valued at more than $500,000, Belvedere properties are even more expensive.

Natural Beauties

To see the Bay Area's last stands of old-growth redwood trees, drive north on California Highway 1 to **Muir Woods National Monument.** Just twelve miles north of the Golden Gate Bridge and located at the foot of Mount Tamalpais, the trees rise to heights of more than 250 feet. Under the two thousand-year-old redwoods is a thriving ecosystem of flowers, ferns, and lichen, with salamanders, chipmunks, deer, and birds its most frequently seen inhabitants. Six miles of walking trails wind through the 560-acre state park and national monument, offering a cathedrallike serenity with only the sounds of the creeks and birdcalls to break the silence.

Commercial bus tours to Muir Woods and Sausalito last from about three to three and a half hours and cost around $28 for adults, and half-price for children 5 to 11. They include a stroll through the woods and a short stop in Sausalito. Tours that also have Alcatraz on the itinerary last two hours longer and cost about $40 for adults and $20 for children 5 to 11 (you'll frequently find $3 discount coupons for these tours).

If you have $35 to spend ($49.95 including lunch) and want to take a walking tour of Muir Woods with accurate information on the flora and fauna, Tom's Scenic Walking Tours (510/845-8056) are led by the former chairman of the Sierra Club's steering committee. The tour price includes door-to-door transportation to and from San Francisco, and hikes are from two to four miles long.

Seventy miles north of San Francisco on Highway 1, **Fort Ross** stands on a bluff swept by winds off the Pacific Ocean. The fort was established in 1812 to provide food for the Russian colonies in Alaska (Ross is a shortened form of Rossiya—Russia). Colonists at the fort included twenty-five Russians and eighty Aleuts from the islands of western Alaska who hunted seal and otter from sealskin kayaks. The fort's fourteen-foot redwood walls surround Kuskov House, formerly the Russian-American Company manager's house, two octagonal blockhouses, St. Nicholas Chapel, topped with an Orthodox cross, and more wooden Orthodox crosses marking grave sites in the cemetery. The church is a reconstruction which replaced the original, a 1906 quake victim.

The fort existed under the Russians until 1841, when the lands were sold to John Sutter (gold was discovered near his sawmill in the Mother Lode seven years later). The Russians' attempts at agriculture had not been altogether successful, though grapes and fruit orchards flourished, and the colony's population increased to four hundred.

On Living History Day, held annually in late July, volunteers recreate Fort Ross life in the nineteenth century. Twice a year (Memorial Day and Fourth of July weekends) Russian Orthodox services are conducted in the chapel. During summer months, historical presentations are given three times daily in the fort compound. In winter, they take place twice daily on weekends and at noon on weekdays.

There is a small museum and bookstore in the visitor

center. Since no food is available, bring a picnic—there are tables on the site—if you'll be visiting at lunchtime. Though there is no admission charged per se, there's a $6 per vehicle parking fee ($5 for seniors).

To get to Fort Ross by the fastest route, take Highway 101 north to Petaluma. Exit at Bodega Avenue, which turns into Valley Ford Road. Take Valley Ford Road to the coast, then follow Highway 1 north to Fort Ross (it's twelve miles north of the town of Jenner).

Even farther north, **Point Reyes National Seashore** is a natural for nature lovers, with more than thirty miles of protected coastline, rugged cliffs, vast wetlands, lush forests, and open grasslands. There are three visitor centers at the park. Closest to the highway, the Bear Valley Center provides an orientation to the parks and trails, as well as introduces visitors to area plant and animal species. A short orientation film and slide program may be seen upon request. The center is open Monday through Friday, 9 A.M. to 5 P.M.; weekends and holidays, 8 A.M. to 5 P.M. (415/663-1092).

The Lighthouse Center, located on the Point Reyes Headlands, features exhibits on whales, wildflowers, and lighthouses. The lighthouse itself is three hundred steps down the cliff from the center, which is open Thursday to Monday, 10 A.M. to 5 P.M. (415/669-1534).

Ken Patrick Center, located at Drake's Beach, focuses on sixteenth-century maritime exploration, marine fossils, and marine environments. A 250-gallon saltwater aquarium contains plant and animal life from Drakes Bay. Open weekends and holidays, 10 A.M. to 12 P.M. and 12:30 to 5 P.M.; (415/669-1250).

The free "Point Reyes Trail Guide" divides the twenty hikes, which range in length from .6 to 12 miles, into those of less than one hour, one to three hours, and three to six hours. They're also keyed to indicate difficulty; whether the trail has panoramic views, is wooded or has beach access; if dogs on leash and bicycles are allowed; and whether the trails are wheelchair accessible. Opportunities for tide pooling at low tides, whale watching, birding, and viewing wildflowers (January to April) are also indicated. If you would rather drive, it's possible to go by car to several of the park's attractions—the visitor centers, Sea Lion Overlook, and Point Reyes and Limantour beaches.

Point Reyes also offers some of the finest bird watching in the United States, with more than four hundred avian species observed in the park and its adjacent waters. A free bird-watching guide tells where to go to see pileated woodpeckers, green-backed heron, egrets, peregrine falcons, long-eared owls, and dozens of other species. Visitors can also watch birds being banded at the observatory from April 1 through Thanksgiving.

Jutting ten miles into the ocean, the headlands of Point Reyes offer one of the finest spots along the Pacific Coast from which to view the gray whale migrations. The huge mammals—up to fifty feet long and forty tons in weight— leave Baja, California, in February, and the greatest numbers of them pass by Point Reyes in mid-March. Mother whales and their babies arrive later and swim closer to the shore. The best time to see the whales on their southern migration is from late December to mid-January. Elephant seals begin to arrive at the point in late November and stay until mid-March; they are easy to spot from the cliffs surrounding the lighthouse.

Mendocino–Fort Bragg

My favorite getaway spot is the Mendocino–Fort Bragg area on the coast about eighty miles north of San Francisco. **Mendocino** started out as a lumber town. The 1854 **Ford House** (the only building on the bluff opposite Main Street, Mendocino; 707/937-5397) was the one-time home of the mill's superintendent, his wife, and six children. Now it's a museum with exhibits of the area's history.

The museum's replica of Mendocino in 1890 serves as a good orientation to the town, since many of the buildings stand today. Most of them were erected in 1870 and 1880, but a few are of earlier construction. One of the most interesting, the red and green **Temple of Kwan Tai** (Albion Street) is the oldest original Chinese temple left on the Northern California coast. At one time, Mendocino's Chinese community was large enough to support seven herb shops. Today, only one of the original families remain. Because of the temple's deteriorated condition, it is open only by appointment (707/937-5123).

Fort Bragg is about ten miles north of Mendocino, but because of development along the highway, the distance seems shorter. The **Guest House Museum** (343 North Main Street, Fort Bragg; 707/961-2823) is a three-story Victorian built for the Union Lumber Company's founder. The museum chronicles the forest products industry on the Mendocino Coast, an industry which is still thriving.

Another Fort Bragg industry is fishing, with **Noyo Harbor** home of the local fishing fleet. It is also the place from which sport fishing and whale-watching trips depart.

A free "Walking Tour of Historic Fort Bragg" brochure, indicating thirty-one points of interest, is available from the Fort Bragg–Mendocino Coast Chamber of Commerce (332 N. Main Street, Fort Bragg; 707/961-6300).

One of the area's busiest tourist attractions, the **"Skunk" trains,** operate on the California Western Railroad roadbed that has been in operation for more than a hundred years. In summer, the trains are pulled by "Ole No. 45" Baldwin steam engine. The rest of the year, the job is done by a 1925 MS-100 motorcar, a 1935 MS-300 motorcar, or diesel engine No. 64.

The train's route to the inland town of Willits and back (forty miles each way) is a scenic one, with enough tunnels, trestles, stands of redwoods, switchbacks, rural landscapes, and ocean views to keep Kodak in business. During warm weather there are outdoor observation platforms from which to take your shots. The Skunk depot in Fort Bragg is at

Highway 1 and Laurel Street; 707/964-6371. Full-day trips (round-trip, Fort Bragg to Willits) cost $26 for adults; $12 for children 5 to 11. Halfway trips (Fort Bragg to Northspur and back) cost $21 and $10.

Because the area is a tourist favorite and so many people on vacation like to shop, the stores, boutiques, and galleries are interesting enough to keep even shop-til-they-droppers panting. Some of the items for sale are prohibitively expensive. (One salesperson at Golden Goose, an upscale shop on Mendocino's Main Street, said candidly that they "didn't have any bargains.") But there is enough quality merchandise at reasonable prices that you'll be able to stock up on gifts—both for your friends and yourself.

Among the affordable items at **Fittings for Home and Garden** (45050 Main Street, Mendocino; 707/937-0160) are attractive palm-frond sconces for candles ($8.25 to $30.25), colorful doorman's umbrellas ($27.50), and outdoor water spigots shaped like birds and small animals (various prices).

You'll find great toys as well as telescopes, globes, and binoculars at **Out of This World** (45100 Main Street; 707/937-3335). Meggabubbles, with a Mega bubble wand, tray, and bubble formula, costs $16.98. Solar science kits are $19.98, and model kits of the Parthenon, Taj Mahal, and Leaning Tower of Pisa cost $25 each. Ocean music CDs cost $15.95, and cassettes, $9.95.

In Fort Bragg at **Fuchsiarama** (in the arcade at 401 N. Main; no phone) check out the miniature recreations of Point Loma, Point Cabrillo, and Point Arena lighthouses. Electrically wired, they cost from $14 to $39.

Also in the arcade, **Guatemalan for Now** (707/964-8815) has some quality items from Guatemala at bargain prices, such as embroidered velvet eyeglass cases for less than $15. Coupons frequently available at the chamber of commerce take 20 percent off the price of any item in the store, and half of the proceeds from each item go back to the Guatemalan village where the items were made. The store allegedly got its rather unusual name when one of the owners asked another what they should call the store. "Let's just call it Guatemalan, for now," was the reply.

A lot of creative cooking goes on along the Mendocino Coast, and the results are for sale. At **Mendocino Jams and Preserves** (440 Main Street, Mendocino; 707/937-1037) you can sample the chutneys, jams, marmalades, and dessert toppings before you buy—not to mention items like the orange mustard and pure pistachio butter.

The **Hot Pepper Jelly Company** (530 N. Main Street, Fort Bragg; 800/892-4823) sells everything from cabernet sauvignon and white zinfandel wine jelly to raspberry trifles. Waffle mix and syrup, a variety of vinegars and dressings, crunchy cranberry and fifteen other kinds of mustards, several desserts, coffees, root beer, teas, and, of course, hot pepper jelly round out the product line.

Shopping also reflects the area's artistic bent. **Showcase Gallery** (560 Main Street, Mendocino; 707/937-2829) features fine arts and crafts by Mendocino and Northern California artists. **Northcoast Artists** (362 N. Main Street, Fort Bragg; 707/964-8266) is a cooperative involving twenty-two local artists, including David Ayster, Mariko Irie, and Nansee New. **Highlight Gallery** (45052 Main Street, Mendocino; 707/937-3132) also features the work of several artists.

Though prices can be high for the larger works, they are less expensive than works sold by the same artists through galleries in San Francisco. You'll be able to find an abundance of original art at prices most of us consider to be bargains. The gift shop at the **Mendocino Art Center** (45200 Little Lake Street, Mendocino; 707/937-5818) has pottery bud vases that sell for $7 and handmade earrings for less than $20.

On First Fridays, several Fort Bragg galleries are open, usually from 5:30 to 8 P.M., but sometimes beginning as early as 4 P.M. On the second Saturday of each month, it's the Mendocino galleries' turn. From one to six of the dozen-and-a-half galleries in town are open on any given second Saturday at about the same hours as those in Fort Bragg. Special exhibits often open on these occasions, artists are present, refreshments are served, and there's no charge.

Even more interesting than shopping in the galleries is visiting individual artists in their studios. Some of them are open to the public on a regular basis. Others are accessible only if you are interested in buying something the particular artist has created or in commissioning a work.

At the **Fort Bragg Fabric Studio** (122 E. Fir Street; 707/961-1800), Lolli Jacobsen, Gail Deutsch, and Katharine Bicknell design and produce hand-screened fabrics, garments, and articles for the home (Jacobsen prints scarves for the San Francisco Opera and California Shakespeare Festival while Bicknell's specialty is cotton knit apparel. An enchanting "Dancers Pattern" pillow by Deutsch sells for $40.) At the studio, neckties costs from $28 to $30, T-shirts from $8 to $12, and seconds go for much less.

At **Four Sisters** (400 N. Harrison Street, Fort Bragg; 707/964-4141) three graduates of the renowned James Krenov woodworking course at College of the Redwoods—all of whom were honored by being invited back for additional study—produce museum-quality desks, chairs, tables, chests, and other furniture.

Zida Borcich creates stationery that's sold by Francis Orr in Beverly Hills, Rebecca Moss in New York, and other upscale stores, and her special-order client list reads like *Who's Who*. Her **Zida Borcich Letterpress** (711 N. Main Street, Fort Bragg; 707/964-2522) houses two Heidelberg windmill presses, two one-hundred-year-old Chandler and Price presses, and cases of letterpress ornaments, and letters and numbers in hundreds of typefaces. Her papers are available in San Francisco at **Arch** (47 Jackson Street; 415/433-2724).

Artist **Sev Ickes'** (552 N. Main Street, Fort Bragg; 707/961-0771) naif paintings hang in important collections nationwide. Locally, her work is shown at **Gallery One** (Highway 1 entrance to Mendocino; 707/937-5154).

Although you most likely won't want to carry wooden lawn furniture home, you can inspect the finished products (and see them being made) at **Adirondak Designs** (350 Cypress Street, Fort Bragg; 800/222-2701). The preassembled components are made by developmentally disabled people of all ages. The furniture is top quality and prices are extremely reasonable.

People who are happiest in the great outdoors will probably forgo the area's shopping and man-made attractions in order to explore the state parks along the coast. An eight-mile foot and bicycle path, the sandy beach at Pudding Creek, and whale-watching platform are among the most popular features at MacKerricher State Park, three miles north of Fort Bragg.

Russian Gulch State Park, eight miles south of Fort Bragg and two miles north of Mendocino, offers rocky headlands and scenic hiking trails—one leads to a small waterfall. At **Jug-handle State Reserve,** between MacKerricher and Russian Gulch, the popular "Ecological Staircase Trail" leads through five wave-cut land terraces, result of hundreds of thousands of years of the earth's movement. Each terrace is about one hundred feet higher and one hundred thousand years older than the terrace below it.

Van Damme State Park, three miles south of Mendocino, features a "Discovery Trail" through the Pygmy Forest, home of species of plants that are decades old but only a few feet tall. "The Secrets of Little River" is a one-and-a-half-mile trail marked with ten salmon sculptures. The numbered markers and a companion brochure guide hikers through the life cycle of the coho salmon. Also at Van Damme, the Little River runs into the Pacific, and the beaches are favorites of abalone divers.

Glass Beach, located at the foot of Elm Street in Fort Bragg, was once a public dump. Now it's the place to find glass and pottery worn smooth by the ocean.

Among the area's prime whale-watching spots are the headlands directly opposite Main Street in the village of

TAKE TIME TO SMELL THE ROSES

It's hard to compete with the natural beauty of the Mendocino Coast's vegetation—towering redwoods sheltering lacy ferns, carpets of wildflowers spilling their colors down the cliffs. But somehow the clean air, rich soil, and perfect blend of rain and sunshine make Mendocino's made-by-man gardens grown with unusual beauty, too.

A good place to start your free garden tour is at the forty-seven-acre Mendocino Coast Botanical Garden in Fort Bragg, one of only three botanical gardens in the United States that is situated beside an ocean. Sharing the space with a vegetable garden set in a pioneer orchard is a series of theme gardens— with roses, dahlias, camellias, rhododendrons (the area's signature plant), and other flowers—crisscrossed by paths and creeks. Just north of Fort Bragg, **Fuchsiarama** (23201 N. Highway One, Fort Bragg; 707/964-0429) blooms with every variety of fuchsia.

In Mendocino, the garden of **Cafe Beaujolais** (961 Ukiah Street, Mendocino; 707/937-5614) is such a beauty that the restaurant offers Saturday tours twice monthly in spring and summer. Just south of Mendocino, the gardens of the coast's famous **Heritage House Inn** (5200 N. Highway 1, Little River; 800/235-5885 or 707/937-5885) are also open to the public.

As for those wildflowers, the North Coast Interpretive Association sponsors walks on the Point Cabrillo Lighthouse Preserve from mid-May through September, and docent-led spring wildflower walks on the headlands are offered by the Ford House Visitor Center on Saturdays in April.

Mendocino, Todd's Point at the south end of Fort Bragg, the Point Arena Lighthouse, and the three state parks along the coast—Jughandle, Russian Gulch, and MacKerricher. Whale-watching boat trips that last about one and a half hours cost $20 per person. Half-hour whale-watching flights cost $85 and can accommodate one to three passengers (707/937-1224).

You can rent canoes, kayaks, and bicycles at **Catch a Canoe and Bicycles, Too** (Highway 1 and Compiche-Ukiah Road; 707/937-0273 or 800/320-BIKE). Canoe and kayak rentals for use on the eight-mile-long Little River estuary are from $10 to $18 per hour (two-hour minimum) and from $30 to $48 per day. Life jackets, paddles, and instruction are included in the rental fees. Mountain bike rentals are $10 an hour (two-hour minimum) and $25 a day. All rentals, except for parties of eight or more, are on a first-come basis.

Because it's so photogenic, Mendocino has been used through the years for location work by television and movie studios. *East of Eden* is among the sixty or so films that have been shot in the area, and the fictitious Cabot Cove, Maine, in TV's *Murder, She Wrote* is Mendocino in disguise. To find out if any movies or TV shows are being filmed while you're in the Mendocino–Fort Bragg area, just ask at the chamber of commerce in Fort Bragg.

Many people who move to Mendocino–Fort Bragg—and those numbers are growing—fall in love with the area while on vacation and create lives that allow them to become permanent residents. Some become bed and breakfast proprietors, some establish businesses which cater to tourists.

Less tied to a specific location, artists and musicians by the dozens have been drawn to the Mendocino Coast for decades, creating a cultural scene richer than those usually found in more populous areas. For example, though Mendocino's population is one thousand and Fort Bragg's is five thousand, the community supports the Gloriana Opera Company (707/964-7469), the Warehouse Repertory Theatre Company (707/937-4477), the Symphony of the Redwoods (707/964-0898) and a variety of instrumental ensembles.

Several concerts by local musicians are presented each year by the **Fort Bragg Center for the Arts** (337 N. Franklin Street, Fort Bragg; 707/937-0807). The annual Mendocino Music Festival (707/937-2044), which takes place during twelve days in July in a huge tent on the headlands, features symphonic productions as well as jazz, blues, opera, and dance.

The community calendar of events is crowded, to say the least. Annual events range from an Amnesty International yard sale in July to the Great Rubber Ducky Race in May. There are two whale festivals, candlelight bed and breakfast inn tours during the holiday season, pancake breakfasts, craft fairs, parades, and church bazaars.

Several free publications describe area attractions and tell what's going on. One of them, the *Mendocino County Directory*, even includes tide tables for each month of the year. The best selection of these publications is available at the **Mendocino–Fort Bragg Chamber of Commerce** (332 N. Main Street, Fort Bragg; 707/961-6300).

When it's time for lunch, a good choice is the **Fort Bragg Grille** (356 N. Main Street, Fort Bragg; 707/964-FOOD). The warm spinach salad with a mustard vinaigrette, pecans, white raisins, and roasted red bell pepper pieces is outstanding ($4.95). The custom tossed salads, also $4.95, allow you to choose your own salad base—pasta, rice, greens, or spinach, and as many of the fourteen salad ingredients as you want.

At the **Mendocino Bakery and Cafe** (10485 Lansing Street, Mendocino; 707/937-0836), everything is made from scratch—green chili chicken tamales ($2.75), savory veggie cakes with ginger tamari dipping sauce (two for $3), and a menu of interesting lunch and dinner dishes. The four menu choices at breakfast include granola and yogurt with fresh fruit plate ($4.95) and country breakfast burritos filled with scrambled eggs, country potatoes, and pepperjack cheese ($3.95).

At Cafe Beaujolais (address above) there's a fixed price "Country Menu" on Tuesday, Wednesday, and Thursday nights ($25). A typical meal might be white bean soup with herb pesto, roast free-range chicken with kumquat sauce, prosciutto, and orange gremolata, and frozen raspberry soufflé.

The "Champagne Sunday Brunch" at **Little River Inn** (7751

N. Highway 1; 707/937-5942) features eight menu choices, including Shrimp Louie ($10.50) and ollalieberry blintzes ($7.50) to go along with the complimentary champagne.

All the above provide great meals, but if I could have dinner at one restaurant every night I would choose the **Rendezvous Inn and Restaurant** (647 N. Main Street, Fort Bragg; 707/491-8142). It stacks up well against any restaurant in San Francisco, New York, or Paris, and costs much less than most of them.

Starters include toasted garlic and warm raclette cheese served with baguette slices ($5.25), duck ravioli served with a sweet and sour citrus sauce and crystallized ginger ($4.75), and terrine of wild boar served with huckleberry chutney ($5.25). Among the entrées, there are delicious vegetarian beggar's purses ($15.95), jambalaya ($14.25), and some wonderful pasta dishes $11.75 to $12.75) as well as more exotic fare.

By all means, save room for dessert (all at $4). The bread pudding is served with a whiskey-raisin sauce. The double caramel custard pairs a caramel flavored custard with a light caramel sauce, and the Chocolate Marquise is a dense chocolate mousse served with a lovely orange sauce. Incidentally, the Rendezvous was one of 261 restaurants worldwide to win an Award of Excellence from *Wine Spectator* in 1996. Some of the wines, which are mostly in the mid-price range, are also sold by the half bottle and glass. Dinner is served Wednesday through Sunday.

There's really no one best time to visit Mendocino–Fort Bragg. The most perfect days, as far as temperature is concerned, are in spring and fall. Days in summer can be equally fine (but generally there are more people around), and the misty, high-fog days make the landscape look like a scene out of *Brigadoon*. For people who enjoy the drama of blustery days with a pounding surf or crisp sunny weather, winter is the time to stay.

The fastest route to Mendocino–Fort Bragg from San Francisco follows Highway 101 across the Golden Gate Bridge

SAMPLING THE BEDS AND BREAKFASTS

To fully do justice to the Mendocino–Fort Bragg area, you really should spend a night or two, especially if you enjoy staying in bed and breakfast establishments.

There's something about beds with ruffled pillowcases and breakfast served on bone china with orange juice in cut-glass goblets that gets vacation mornings off to a marvelous start. And the assortment of B and Bs along the Mendocino Coast assures that there are one or more to suit every traveler's taste.

My idea of the ultimate is the **Whitegate Inn** (499 Howard Street, Mendocino; 707/937-4892 or 800/531-7282). The public rooms and six guest rooms in the impeccably restored 1880s Victorian are furnished with quality antiques, and the gardens surrounding the house and gazebo brim with wisteria, primroses, clematis, and jasmine.

Breakfasts are elegant, with table settings accented by one-of-a-kind antique napkin rings. Among the house specialties are caramel-apple French toast and pecan date pancakes. Through the day, there are crisp apples and home-baked chocolate chip cookies to munch on, along with an endless supply of bottled mineral water. In the afternoon, tea, wine, and hors d'oeuvres are set out for guests to enjoy.

The Whitegate Inn is located on a quiet side street just a block from the Mendocino Headlands and not much farther from the shops downtown. Rates range from $99 to $169 on weekdays; $139 to $189 on weekends, holidays, and during all of July through October. However, from December through April on Monday through Thursday nights, selected rooms go for half price—a terrific bargain.

A compelling feature of **Little River Inn** (7751 N. Highway 1; 707/937-5942) is its location overlooking the ocean. It is also connected by hiking trails to adjacent Van Damme State Park. Built in 1853 by Silas Coombs, the inn is operated by his great grandchildren. Double-room rates are $85 to $255, depending on amenities (you can get rooms with two queen beds and a terrific ocean view for $115).

Guests at the **Grey Whale Inn** (615 North Main Street, Fort

Bragg; 707/964-0640 or 800/382-7244) can join owner Colette Bailey for all or part of her daily seven-mile jaunt to Mackerricher State Park and back—especially interesting from December to April, when the gray whales are migrating. Double rooms at the Grey Whale Inn go from $99 to $165, with special "Whale of a Rate" deals during whale-watching season.

Though not a bed and breakfast, the 1878 **Mendocino Hotel** (45080 Main Street; 707/937-0511 or 800/548-0513) has the same sort of ambience. Rooms are decorated with antiques, and some of them look out on the Mendocino Coast. A printed description of the antiques in the hotel's lobby, dining room, and bar is available. (Ask at the front desk. The hotel's newer garden suites, which occupy the block behind the hotel, are especially pleasing.) Rooms and suites range in price from $65 to $225.

Complete listings of area bed and breakfasts are included in several free publications available from the Fort Bragg–Mendocino Coast Chamber of Commerce.

---

to Cloverdale, then goes northwest through the Alexander Valley on Highway 128 to just south of Albion, where it joins Highway 1. Mendocino is about six miles, and Fort Bragg about sixteen miles, north of Albion. The beauty of the Alexander Valley, with its villages and vineyards, is worth the trip in itself, especially on a misty morning as the sun breaks through.

The Grape Vine Trail

One of the most popular day trips from San Francisco is to the California Wine Country. Although wine is grown in a number of areas throughout the state, it's the Sonoma and Napa valleys (as well as vineyards in adjacent but less densely cultivated Anderson and Alexander valleys) that are known as Wine Country. It's very difficult to cover both the Napa and Sonoma valleys very thoroughly in one day, but it can be done by driving up one, crossing over on Calistoga Road or Trinity Road and driving down the other.

On a good day—Wednesday and Thursday are usually the best—it takes about an hour and a half to drive from San Francisco to the heart of the Wine Country. On a bad day you can spend three or four hours traveling the same route. Weekends from June through October should be avoided unless you don't mind throngs of people and nonstop traffic once you get to the valleys.

It is possible to visit the Wine Country without a car, by taking a ferry between San Francisco and Vallejo ($7.50 for adults one-way; $6 for seniors and people 13 to 18; $4 for children 4 to 12) then using the Route 10 Napa Valley Transit buses. One-way bus fares between Vallejo and Calistoga (the terminus of the route) are $2.50 for adults; $1.80 for students between 6 and 18 years, and $1.25 for seniors over 65. While in Napa Valley, you can use the transit system to go from one town to the next.

Several companies offer commercial bus tours to the area. One nine-hour Napa Valley tour, with a winery tour and tasting, shopping, a museum visit in Calistoga, and the return drive through the valley with a second winery visit costs $42 for adults and $21 for children 5 to 11. Lunch is not included in the price.

A six-hour tour to the Sonoma Valley includes a winery tour, tastings at two wineries, and a stop in the town of Sonoma to visit the historic districts and/or shopping. The tour, which does not include lunch, costs $37 for adults and $18.50 for children 5 to 11.

If there are two or more people in your party, the most economical way to take the trip is by car. During your stay, there are several rather expensive things you might do—hot-air balloon rides, jeep tours along the backroads, dining excursions on the Napa Valley Wine Train—but chances are you'll find enough exciting low- or no-cost activities to fill your stay, whether its for a few hours or a few days.

The best way to absorb the Wine Country's essence is by hiking or riding a bicycle down its vineyard roads. At **St. Helena Cyclery** (1156 Main Street, St. Helena; 707/963-7736) bikes rent for $7 an hour, $25 a day. Included in the rental charge are a helmet, lock, water bottle cage, rear rack, and bag for carrying picnic supplies. Maps and tour information are also available. The Cyclery is open Monday through Saturday from 9:30 A.M. to 9:30 P.M., and Sunday 10 A.M. to 5 P.M.

Speaking of picnics, if you're "A loaf of bread, a jug of wine" kind of picnicker, you'll find wine easily, and you can get the bread at the **Model Bakery,** at 1357 Main Street in St. Helena (707/963-8192). Breads baked daily—sweet and sourdough French, *pain du vin,* cracked wheat, walnut, *fougasse* and *ciabatta*—are for sale, as well as special breads such as black olive levain and buckwheat raisin. Buy a couple of cookies, too. Their specialty is the Chocolate Rad, but I like the oatmeal raisin and the white chocolate chip hazelnut cookies better. The cookies are huge and cost $1.50 each.

For a more extensive array of picnic supplies, you'll want to go to the **Napa Valley Olive Oil Manufacturing Company,** housed in a former barn where olives were pressed (Charter Oak Avenue; 707/963-4173) or **V. Sattui Winery** (White Lane at California Highway 29; 707/963-7714) with more than two hundred different cheeses, house-made salads, pâtés, meats, and desserts. Both of these shops are in St. Helena.

A bike path goes all the way from the town of Napa to beyond Calistoga at the head of the Napa Valley. The bike path through Sonoma Valley begins along California Highway 37 and goes through the town of Sonoma to the outskirts of Santa Rosa. In addition to the bicycle paths, many of the off-highway roads in the valleys are great for bicycling, with little traffic and picturesque views wherever you look. If you want to cross from one valley to the other, Calistoga Road is easier than Trinity Road, which is usually only attempted by cyclists with thighs as big as tree trunks.

Pine Ridge Winery (5901 Silverado Trail; 707/253-7500) in

Napa Valley features a free fifty-acre mountain biking park with four miles of hiking and class-one mountain bike trails through terraced vineyards. Also on Silverado Trail, Clos du Val Wine Company, at no. 5330 (707/252-6711) has a picnic area complete with bike racks.

A free winery map and historic walking tour guide are available at the **Sonoma Valley Chamber of Commerce** (645 Broadway, Sonoma; 707/996-1033). The walking tour includes sixty points of interest, most within an eight-block area.

For most visitors, a winery map is necessary if they're looking for particular brands of wine. The most helpful guides are those that give information about tours, such as the free "Spotlight's Wine Country Guide." Whereas most of the larger wineries are open to the public seven days a week, and many of them offer free tours, others do not. And unlike a decade ago, when just about every winery offered free tastes, many of them now charge for wine tasting.

Among the wineries that offer both **free tours and tasting** in the Napa Valley are **Beaulieu Vineyards** (1960 St. Helena Highway; 707/963-2411) from 10 A.M. to 5 P.M. and **Beringer Vineyard** (2000 Main Street, St. Helena; 707/963-7115) from 9:30 A.M. to 5 P.M. daily. In Sonoma Valley, **Sebastiani Vineyards** (389 4th Street East; 707/938-5532), four blocks from Sonoma's plaza offers tours and tasting from 10 A.M. to 4 P.M. daily.

You can also watch cheese being made at the **Sonoma Cheese Factory** on the plaza and sample its Sonoma Jack cheese from 9:30 A.M. to 5:30 P.M. daily.

For more complete information about the wineries, get a copy of the wine edition of the *St. Helena Star* (2328 Main Street; 707/963-2731), which comes out in October and contains a compendium of the more than two hundred wineries in the Napa Valley. Most of the wineries are small, family-owned operations that make only a few thousand cases of wine a year, in contrast to the giant Sutter Home, which produces about six and a half million cases.

As far as I'm concerned, the three most interesting communities are St. Helena and Calistoga in the Napa Valley and Sonoma in the Sonoma Valley.

I like St. Helena because it is such a pretty little town and is the most fun for shopping. Also, for anyone in a splurgy mood, it is the place in the Wine Country to have dinner. Several of its restaurants, including **Terra** (1345 Railroad Avenue; 707/963-8931), **Tra Vigne Restaurant** (1050 Charter Oak Avenue; 707/963-4444) and the **Restaurant at Meadowood** (900 Meadowood Lane; 707/963-3646)—as well as the **French Laundry** in neighboring Yountville (6640 Washington Street; 707/944-2380)—are nationally recognized.

As far as St. Helena's shops are concerned, don't miss **On the Vine** (1234 Main Street; 707/963-2209), which showcases grape-themed wearable art, jewelry, and housewares. There are earrings made of semiprecious stones and 24-karat gold vermeil over sterling silver and shaped like bunches of grapes ($38 a pair), pewter business card holders with burnished brass grape clusters as their decoration ($38), and hand-painted scarves, paperweights, perfume flasks, and picture frames.

Even if you're not in the market for a "Field of Grapes" silk jacket ($725) or a silk cummerbund in a pattern of plump purple grapes ($240; with matching bow tie, $340), you'll enjoy looking around this ultra-special shop.

The **Gallery on Main Street** (1359 Main Street; 707/963-3350) features multi-plate etchings by Gail Packer. Signed, numbered, and with specially made frames, prices start at $400. Among the other area artists represented are watercolorist Dorie Tuttle, landscape painter Josh Adams, and Ray Voisard, who is best known for his local scenes.

You can watch candles being handcrafted at **Hurd Beeswax Candles** (3020 St. Helena Highway North; 707/963-7201). Shaped like flowers, swirled into inverted icicles, or traditionally fashioned, the candles are produced at the Freemark Abbey Winery, so you can buy your candlelight and wine all in one place.

Down the road at Yountville, **RAKU Ceramic Collection** (707/944-9424) and **RASberry's Art Glass** (707/944-9211), both at Beard Plaza, are two shops that people interested in fine housewares will want to visit.

Taking the Waters—and the Mud

At the top of the Napa Valley, the town of Calistoga can be good for what ails you—especially if you have aches and pains. The story is that California's first millionaire, Sam Brannan, observed the local Indians bathing in the mineral-laden mud some 150 years ago and realized it had therapeutic qualities.

Since that time, hundreds of thousands of people have journeyed to the little town to take the waters and immerse themselves in mud. Now there are more than a dozen spas which offer mineralized mud baths, hot mineral pools, massage, and more recent innovations such as aromatherapy, herbal facials, and reflexology.

The mud baths and other treatments don't come cheap, but you can easily find coupons that, along with $72, will buy mud baths for two people or take 10 percent off other treatments. And while you're in the Calistoga area, you may want to check out Calistoga's geyser (one mile north of town on Tubbs Lane between California highways 29 and 128), which erupts every forty minutes. Admission is $5 for adults, $4 for people over 60, and $2 for those 6 to 12.

Near the base of the Sonoma Valley, the town of Sonoma is one of California's historically important spots. In fact, it was capital of the independent Republic of California for twenty-five tumultuous days in 1846 following the Bear Flag Revolt. To learn about its role in the Golden State's early history, you can take a self-guided tour of **Sonoma State Historic Park,** centerpiece of which is Sonoma Plaza in the heart of town (20 E. Spain Street; 707/938-1519).

Thirteen points of interest are located in and around the

plaza, laid out by General Mariano Guadalupe Vallejo in 1835, when the area was part of Mexico. Among the most interesting buildings fronting on the plaza is General Vallejo's home. Although there's no admission fee to the historic district, it costs $2 for adults and $1 for children ages 6 to 12 to tour the home. Guided tours are conducted Monday through Friday.

Also among the historic buildings, **Mission San Francisco Solano de Sonoma** was the last of the twenty-one missions to be built by the Franciscan padres in California, marking the northern end of El Camino Real (The King's Highway). The mission is open daily, 10 A.M. to 5 P.M. (707/938-0510). Admission to the Vallejo home also includes the entry fee to the mission.

One of Sonoma Valley's best-loved beauty spots is **Glen Ellen,** about seven miles north of Sonoma, where Jack London settled in 1913. Jack London State Historic Park is on the site of the author's "Beauty Ranch" (open 8 A.M. to sunset, $5 per car). A museum in the park contains London memorabilia (10 A.M. to 5 P.M.).

While you're in the valley, be on the lookout for promotions such as the 1997 Sonoma Valley Super Savers Card, which offers discounts on lodging, dining, wine, and merchandise at participating businesses.

Weather in the Wine Country is pleasant most of the year. Typically, two-thirds of the days are clear, and average rainfall, which occurs primarily during the winter months, is thirty-three inches. The range between average maximum and minimum temperatures is only 11 degrees in summer, fall, and winter, and 14 degrees in spring. Average maximum temperature in summer is 92 degrees; in winter, 72 degrees.

If you plan to stay overnight in the Wine Country, be prepared to pay San Francisco rates. Two of the nicest properties are the French country-style **Vineyard Country Inn** (201 Main Street, St. Helena; 707/963-1000) and the delightful **Sutter Home Inn and Carriage House** (277 St. Helena Highway South; 707/963-3104), complete with fireplaces, expanded continental breakfast, and complimentary wine.

Although rooms at the inns in both Napa and Sonoma valleys charge their top rates during the summer and the autumn grape harvest, they're often substantially lower during the rest of the year. Rooms at the venerable **Sonoma Mission Inn and Spa** in Sonoma Valley go for as much as $250 during high season, but can be as low as $110 November through March. For an additional $35, guests can use the spa (steam room, sauna, exercise equipment, and natural hot artesian mineral water swimming pool and whirlpool) and attend fitness classes.

12

Day Trips
and Excursions:
East and South

Heading East

It is eighty-seven miles from San Francisco to Sacramento by the heavily traveled direct route, Interstate Highway 80. It will take longer, but for a delightful change of pace you can drive to California's capital city via the Sacramento River delta. Take I-80 only as far as its intersection with California Highway 4, which you'll follow to California Highway 160 and delta country.

You'll drive atop high levee roads, along water all the way. Valley spreads from earlier days, with their pear orchards and wooden water towers, pleasure craft on the river, and little towns along the riverbank, will provide you with a series of postcard-pretty scenes and glimpses of California as it looked sixty years ago. Especially interesting is the town of **Locke,** which was a Chinese settlement in the early 1900s. Rail fans may want to detour to the outdoor **Sacramento Northern Railway Museum** north of Rio Vista, especially on weekends when the trains are running.

Once you're in the capital city, head for Old Sacramento, the riverfront area where the city's first buildings were erected. (If you're coming from San Francisco on the freeway, turn off I-80 at Interstate Highway 5, then take the Old Sacramento exit.)

A walking guide of Old Sacramento (free at the visitor information center on 2nd Street; 916/447-7644) takes you past the **Lady Adams Building,** the oldest structure remaining in Old Sacramento; Sacramento Engine Company no. 3, which now houses one of the city's top restaurants, and the riverboat *Delta King,* which carried passengers and cargo between San Francisco and Sacramento from 1926 to 1941. In 1984, the *Delta King* was restored as a floating hotel.

Other landmarks include the **Dingley Spice and Coffee Mill,** whose thrifty owner tapped the steam line of the city waterworks to run his machinery (he was eventually caught) and the B. F. Hastings Building, western terminus of the **Pony Express.** Many of the old buildings now contain specialty shops, such as Old City Kites and World of Clowns, where you'll find puppets, porcelain, pictures, pencils, and dozens of other items with circus motifs. At the public market along the riverbank, there's a stall where Asian specialties are sold, a bakery, and produce and flower stands.

Also in Old Sacramento, the **California State Railroad Museum** is touted to be "the largest and finest in North America." The impeccably restored locomotives include Engine No. 60, *Jupiter,* which hauled Pullman cars between Reno and Virginia City, Nevada, during the state's great silver mining days, and Engine No. 21, which was used in the filming of the movie *Union Pacific* and was exhibited at both the Chicago and New York World's Fairs.

Also on display is the opulent "Gold Coast" parlor car, lavishly furnished with brocade armchairs, crystal chandeliers, and a formal dining room. The car was formerly owned by columnist and gourmet Lucius Beebe. The reconstructed Central Pacific passenger depot, located on Front Street between I and J streets, is a part of the museum, too.

The museum is open daily, 10 A.M. to 5 P.M. Admission is $5

for adults, $3 for children ages 6 to 12. Steam trains operate hourly from 10 A.M. to 5 P.M., April through September. In winter, diesel trains run on the first full weekend of December through March, hourly from 12 to 3 P.M.

One-hour sight-seeing cruises along the Sacramento River on the Victorian paddlewheeler *Matthew McKinley* leave from an Old Sacramento dock. The cruise costs $10 for adults and $5 for children under 12 (916/552-2933 or 800/433-0263).

You can easily spend an entire day in Old Sacramento. However, there are several other attractions in the city that you might want to visit as well. Ford automobile fanciers won't want to miss the Towe Ford Museum, with its collection that includes every year and model produced by the Ford Motor Company between 1903 and 1953. Some of the vehicles are originals in excellent condition; others have been authentically restored (2200 Front Street; 916/442-6802). Open daily, 10 A.M. to 6 P.M.; admission is $5 for adults; $4.50 for seniors; $2.50, 14 to 18, and $1, 5 to 13.

Just a few blocks from Old Sacramento, the **California State capitol** is an imposing gold-domed structure which was completed in 1874. It's surrounded by Capitol Park, acres of palm-shaded gardens containing four hundred varieties of plants from around the world.

It's easy to find your way around central Sacramento, since the streets with letters for their names run east and west, while intersecting numbered streets go north and south. A free downtown shuttle makes its rounds every ten to fifteen minutes, stopping at points between Old Sacramento and the Sacramento Convention Center.

Crocker Art Museum (216 O Street; 916/264-5423) features nineteenth- and twentieth-century California art, as well as works by da Vinci, Holbein, Michelangelo, and Rembrandt. The museum's permanent collection is augmented by such visiting exhibits as "Kings and Queens and Soup Tureens," which showcased seventy-one choice objects from the bygone days of elegant dining. Open 10 A.M. to 5 P.M. Wednesday to

Sunday, admission is $4.50 for adults and $2 for visitors 7 to 17 years old.

Sutter's Fort Historic Park (27th and L streets; 916/445-4422) is a favorite with elementary school children. The fort, which offered protection for Sutter's lands and livestock, is formed in a quadrangle with eighteen-foot-high ivy-covered walls surrounding it. The restored adobe buildings contain furniture, clothing, mining tools, and other mementos of early California.

Self-guided audio tours explain the exhibits, which include a bakery, a cooper's shop, a dining room, living quarters, a blacksmith shop, and livestock area. Open daily, 10 A.M. to 5 P.M. Admission is $2 for adults and $1 for people 18 years and under.

Adjacent to the fort is the **California State Indian Museum** (2618 K Street; 916/324-0971), where you can learn about the mythology, feather work, basketry, dances, and ceremonies of the tribes that roamed California before the days of the white man. Open daily, 10 A.M. to 5 P.M.; admission is $2 for adults; $1 for children 6 to 12.

Among other Sacramento attractions from the past are the **Tiffany stained glass windows** at St. Paul's Episcopal Church (15th and J streets; 916/446-2620), the Victorian houses along the tree-lined streets in the area bounded by 7th, 16th, I, and E streets, and the historic city cemetery at 10th Street and Broadway (916/264-5621), the last resting place of early notables, including Mark Hopkins and John Sutter. Free guided tours are offered at 10 A.M. Saturday and Sunday, from May to September.

Among present attractions, the **California Almond Growers plant** (1701 C Street; 916/446-8439)—the largest in the world—offers free twenty-five-minute video programs that show how the nuts are gathered, processed, and made into all kinds of treats. And if you haven't spent all your shopping money in Old Sacramento, you might want to head for the tile-roofed Town and Country Shopping Center at the corner of Marconi and Fulton, where you'll find **William Glen** (916/485-3000), one of the most outstanding housewares stores in the country because of both the variety and quality of its merchandise.

The biggest annual event in the capital city is the **Sacramento Jazz Festival,** which takes place at the end of May. The best months to visit Sacramento are February through July and mid-September through early November. During winter, valley fogs plague the area for several days at a time, and in late summer, temperatures can sizzle at more than 100 degrees, though some days during those periods are near perfect.

The Mother Lode

The golden chain of California's nineteenth-century mining centers stretches for about three hundred miles along the Sierra Nevada foothills. But the most interesting part goes from Nevada City in the north to Sonora, about 140 miles south. All of the towns are within a long day-trip's range of San Francisco.

One of the brightest nuggets in the chain, **Nevada City,** is about fifty-four miles northeast of Sacramento. Established in 1849 and known as the Showcase of the Mother Lode, the town weathered three major fires, economic boom, and bust. At one time during the golden years it was the third largest city in California.

Wherever you wander in this picture-pretty place, you'll see remainders of the past—brick buildings topped by ornate cornices, white picket fences, and wrought-iron grillwork surrounding dignified Victorians with old-fashioned gardens of snapdragons, geraniums, dahlias, and rose bushes. The **National Hotel** (211 Broad Street; 916/265-4551) was built between 1854 and 1856, and is the oldest continuously operating hotel in the state.

At the *Nevada City Chamber of Commerce* (132 Main Street; 916/265-2692), you can buy "The Compleat Pedestrian's Partially Illustrated Guide to Greater Nevada City or Romping Around a Gold Rush Metropolis," by Robert M. Wyckoff. The softcover book ($6) outlines five walking tours and includes additional information, such as a description of how to operate a hydraulic mining gadget called the Monitor, as well as anecdotes about Nevada City's early settlers. It also gives advice on where not to go: "There is a trail to the top but you wouldn't want to take it—the path is filled with poison oak and rattlesnakes. Besides, it's private property and there's a barbed wire fence blocking the trail."

The **Marshall Gold Discovery State Historic Park** (916/622-3470), one of the Gold Country's leading attractions, is on California Highway 49 at Coloma, between Auburn and Placerville. The 275-acre park where James Marshall discovered gold on January 24, 1848, contains several of the town's original buildings, period stores, a museum, gold-mining equipment, and a fully operational replica of John Sutter's sawmill, which stood close to the discovery site.

One of the most interesting buildings is the **Wah Hop Store,** a windowless stone building with a dirt floor where the Oriental population of Coloma shopped. On the shelves are coolie hats, tin boxes of tea, and enamel cooking utensils. An artificial pig and a brace of fowl hang from the rafters, and there's an abacus on the counter that was used to tally customers' bills.

Picnic tables on the grounds are shaded by black locust, persimmon, catalpa, and other trees planted by homesick miners to remind them of the communities they left behind.

The park is at its most exciting on Gold Discovery Anniversary Day (January 24), Historic Demonstration Day (the second Saturday in June), the U.S. National Gold Panning Championships (the first weekend in October), and Christmas in Coloma (varying dates in December). At these events, volunteers recreate gold rush life with demonstrations of cooking, carpentry, gunsmithing, and gold panning, as well as other 1850s-era crafts and skills. Admission to the park is $5 per vehicle.

Eight miles beyond Coloma on Highway 49 is **Placerville** (forty-one miles from Sacramento via U.S. Highway 50), called Hangtown in its early days because of the frequency with which outlaws were strung up. You can get a free map at the **El Dorado County Chamber of Commerce** (542 Main Street, Placerville; 916/621-5885 or 800/547-6279) that will show you such architectural treasures as the Victorian Combellack House, the Episcopal Church of Our Savior (1865), and Stone House, the only remaining building of the town's large Chinese community. Built on hand-hewn rock, the two-story building was, according to one account, the shop of a Chinese herbalist. According to another, the first floor was devoted to opium and gambling, while upstairs was a heavily patronized bordello.

At the **El Dorado County Historical Museum** on the fairgrounds west of the city (100 Placerville Drive; 916/621-5865), the outstanding exhibit is a recreated general store, complete with antique food, tobacco, spice tins, weighing scales, jars of homemade pickles, and a mannequin shopkeeper. The museum is open Wednesday through Saturday, 10 A.M. to 4 P.M.; also Sunday, 10 A.M. to 3:30 P.M., March through October. No admission is charged, but donations are welcome.

The farther south you go along the Golden Chain, the more crowds you encounter—especially on weekends. At Sutter Creek, you can take a self-guided tour past the town's historic buildings and browse the antique stores. A few miles south, at Jackson, the **Amador County Museum** occupies a nine-teenth-century home filled with period antiques. **Culture Connection** (171 Main Street; 209/223-5037), carries items from around the world—shirts from Thailand, and drums from Africa. The hands-down winner for good-tasting, no-nonsense food is **Rosebud's Classic Cafe** (26 Main Street;

APPLE EXTRAVAGANZA

Okay. So you've been in San Francisco lots of times and gone on day trips and excursions to just about everywhere. But have you ever been to **Apple Hill?** It's a fifteen-mile stretch of rolling orchards just east of Placerville and north of Highway 50 where, from September through December, more than forty apple growers sell their fruit—in crates, bushel baskets, and bags—at bargain prices.

Each apple ranch has its own apple specialties: jellies, cider, doughnuts, and pies; apple crepes, dumplings, turnovers, strudel, and candy apples. There are applesauce cookies, apple cakes, apple bars, and apple fritters. If you need ideas on what to cook with the apples you couldn't resist buying, you can buy three different books full of apple recipes compiled by the Apple Hill Growers (phone 916/644-7692 for order forms).

Some of the growers set up wooden stands beside their driveways. Others have year-round showrooms with gift shops and all sorts of apple-themed items for sale—dolls with heads made of dried apples, aprons with big red apple pockets, and apple-shaped cookie jars, pencil holders, and paperweights.

There's trout fishing at one ranch, a miniature train at another. Maps that indicate the locations of the individual apple growing operations are available at the El Dorado County Chamber of Commerce in Placerville (address above).

Incidentally, seventeen different varieties of apples are grown in Apple Hill orchards, so remember that while an apple a day may keep the doctor away, eating seventeen of them while you're at Apple Hill isn't a very good idea.

209/223-1035). In the Jackson area, **Daffodil Hill** (three miles north of the little town of Volcano) is a vision of yellow flowers from March to mid-April.

About eight miles south of Jackson, Mokulemne Hill is a great place for quiet Sunday morning walks. Mok Hill's **Leger Hotel** (across from the firehouse on the town's main drag;

209/286-1401), which dates back to 1852, was recently given a complete renovation. There's a pleasant small garden with swimming pool in the back, and watching the stars of the summer sky through the open, screenless guest room windows is pure delight.

Next tourist center down the line, Angel's Camp, is at its liveliest in May, when the **Jumping Frog Jubilee,** inspired by Mark Twain's "The Celebrated Jumping Frog of Calaveras County," takes place.

Columbia, which was the richest gold town of them all, is a state historic park where you can ride a stagecoach ($4, adults; $3.50, 5 to 12; riding shotgun costs an additional dollar), sip a sarsaparilla, watch a play at the **Fallon House Theater** ($15, adults; $14, over 62; $8, students with ID), and pan for gold ($3). It will cost you much less, however, to wander around admiring the buildings in the twelve-square-block area that was Columbia's business district. The park is open daily, 10 A.M. to 5 P.M., and admission is free.

Four miles south in the busy town of Sonora, the 1857 courthouse and jail now houses the **Toulumne County Museum** (158 W. Bradford Avenue; 209/532-1317). The museum is open daily from 10 A.M. to 4 P.M., Tuesday through Saturday. It's also open Sunday, 10 A.M. to 3:30 P.M., from Memorial Day to Labor Day. No admission is charged, but donations are accepted.

From 1987 through the year 2000, you can expect a number of additional events to take place throughout the Mother Lode, commemorating the California Gold Discovery to Statehood Sesquicentennial (150th anniversary). Historical reenactments, living history demonstrations, gold-panning competitions, and a variety of other special programs are on the Sesquicentennial's calendar.

The Lake in the Sky

Lake Tahoe is a stunner. No doubt about it. Considered to be one of the most beautiful alpine lakes in the world, Tahoe straddles the Nevada-California border with seventy-two miles of shoreline. At an altitude of 6,229 feet, it holds enough water to cover the entire state of California to a depth of fourteen inches.

Around its perimeter are lakeside communities with T-shirt shops and trendy boutiques; cottages and mansions along the shore; neon-trimmed casinos at Stateline and on the Nevada north shore; and natural areas where sometimes you can spot deer.

On the west side of the lake at the U.S. Forest Service Visitor Center, an interpretive trail winds past groves of quaking aspen, across little creeks, and through a meadow of wildflowers to the Stream Profile Chamber, which allows viewers to examine Thomas Creek at eye level. The stream is especially interesting during the kokanee salmons' mating season, when males develop jutting jaws and their heads turn bright red. The area is open daily, 8 A.M. to 5 P.M. from mid-June through September; from 8 A.M. to 5 P.M. Saturday and Sunday the rest of the year (weather permitting). Admission is free.

At the **Pope-Baldwin Recreation Area** (Tallac Historic Site), a few miles south, you can meander on a self-guided tour past mansions where the wealthy spent their summers at the turn of the century (maps are available at the visitor center, open daily, dawn to dusk, from Memorial Day weekend to Labor Day with no admission charge; 916/541-4975 or 573-2674). Various jazz, bluegrass, and chamber music concerts take place in and around the mansions during warm weather months.

The **Ehrman Mansion at Sugar Pint Point State Park** (916/525-7982) houses early artifacts from the Tahoe Basin (admission is $5 per private vehicle; $4 for those operated by people over 62 years), while **Vikingsholm Castle** (916/525-7277), open only during July and August, is considered one of the finest examples of Scandinavian architecture in the western United States. The thirty-eight-room replica of a Norse castle is a one-mile downhill hike from the highway (not to mention the uphill climb back), but it's worth every step. Admission is $2, adults; $1, ages 6 to 18, and free tours are conducted on the hour from 11 A.M. to 4 P.M. Vikingsholm fronts on Emerald Bay, a gorgeous body of water whose color is the same green as the gemstone for which it was named.

Next to the Truckee River in Tahoe City, the **Gatekeeper's Log Cabin Museum** holds the North Lake Tahoe Historical Society's collection of memorabilia, which documents the lake's early history (916/538-1762; open daily 11 A.M. to 5 P.M., June 15 to Labor Day; Wednesday to Sunday, 11 A.M. to 5 P.M., May 1 to June 14, and the day after Labor Day to October 1; free admission). Indian baskets and tools, jewelry, clothing, and photos of early logging and railroad days, as well as souvenirs from the 1960 Winter Olympics, are among the items you'll find in this small museum. The building housed a gatekeeper who kept daily records of the water's level and rate of flow back in the days when logs were sent downstream to sawmills on the lower reaches of the Truckee.

Fanny Bridge at Tahoe City is another great place to stretch your legs and watch the giant trout swimming in the water below. It's also where you rent rubber rafts for drifting down the Truckee River. When you see all the tourists hanging over the rail, you'll understand how the bridge got its name.

Far less developed than the rest of the lakeshore, the east side of Tahoe consists largely of open stretches of beach. If you enjoy looking at spectacular lakefront homes, you will have your best chance of doing so by following Lakeshore Drive at Incline Village. Although there are many showplaces that cost millions of dollars around the lake, those on Lakeshore Drive are the most accessible.

The centerpiece of the **Ponderosa Ranch,** an amusement center near Incline Village, is the legendary home of the Cartwright family on the *Bonanza* TV series. Antique carriages, farm equipment, a wedding chapel, and a recreated western street make kids happy with the ranch, but leave some grownups yawning. The ranch is open daily from 9:30

A.M. to 5 P.M., May to October. Admission is $8.50 for adults, $5.50 for children 5 to 11.

South of the Ponderosa, **Sand Harbor** has the reputation of being Lake Tahoe's most beautiful public beach. It's a great picnic spot too, and the setting for summer performances of Shakespeare under the stars.

If you're planning to spend a night or two at Lake Tahoe— and it is truly a destination in its own right—you'll find the largest concentration of motels at the south end of the lake. Three I especially like are **Inn by the Lake** (3300 Lake Tahoe Boulevard, South Lake Tahoe; 916/542-0330 or 800/877-1466; $84 to $148 during high season); **Lakeland Village** (3535 Lake Tahoe Boulevard; 916/544-1685 or 800/822-5969; $85 to $95 doubles and $125 to $140 suites and efficiencies during high season), and **Richardson's Resort** (California Highway 89 at Jameson Beach Road, South Lake Tahoe; 916/541-1801 or 800-544-1801; cottages on the lake from $79). Rates are usually lower at all Lake Tahoe properties during the off-season. And since the perception of when off-season begins and ends varies, it definitely pays to shop around.

Tahoe's summertime temperatures are usually in the 60- to 80-degree (Fahrenheit) range—just right for taking a ride on the *Tahoe Queen* (which docks at the base of Ski Run Boulevard in South Lake Tahoe; $14 for adults, $5 for children 11 and under; 800/238-2463) or the *M. S. Dixie* (docks at Zephyr Cove; $14, adults; $12, over 60; $5 3 to 12 years old; 702/588-3508). These two paddle wheelers ply the southern part of the lake. For mackinaw and trout fishing or wading in the water, try **Nevada Beach** (even gung-ho kids find it chilly at any time of the year).

Spring and fall days are ideal for bicycling on 132 miles of trails that follow parts of the Tahoe shoreline, or hiking the **Tahoe Rim Trail,** which will completely encircle the lake when finished. There are trailheads at Brockway Summit, Tahoe City, Kingsbury Grade, California Highway 89 at Big

Meadows and U.S. Highway 50 at Spooner Summit. You'll find bicycles for rent and information on bike paths at both Tahoe City and South Lake Tahoe.

After the snow falls, the Tahoe Basin is transformed into a winter playground of fifteen downhill and eleven cross-country-ski resorts. Aerial trams are located at **Heavenly Valley** (top of Ski Run Boulevard near Stateline; 702/586-7000; $10 for adults; $6 for children under 12) and **Squaw Valley** (north of Tahoe City off Highway 29 at 1960 Squaw Valley Boulevard; 916/583-6985; $12 for adults; $5 for children).

On the way back to San Francisco, you might want to stop at **Truckee,** less than twenty miles from Tahoe's north shore. Built in the latter half of the nineteenth century, Truckee was a logging and rail center, and many of the old buildings served as boardinghouses for the loggers and railroaders. Or you might want to spend some time at **Donner Memorial State Park,** a mile west of Donner Lake on I-80, with its impressive monument of a pioneer family set on a twenty-two-foot-high pedestal. Inside the park's Emigrant Trail Museum, you'll find exhibits telling the stories of the building of the Central Pacific Railroad over the Sierras and the trials of the members of the ill-fated Donner Party, who were trapped in the mountains during the winter of 1846–47.

If you have to do Lake Tahoe in a day, plan to leave San Francisco at first light, as the drive will take about three and a half hours. You'll see the lake at its very best in April, May, September, and the first part of October. On weekends in summer traffic is heavy, especially along the south and west shores of the lake.

Don't even attempt the trip from November through February if it's raining in San Francisco. During that part of the year, if it's raining in The City, it's almost always snowing in the Sierras, so you'll have to contend with chains, driving in blizzards, and taking the chance that I-80 will close.

The San Francisco Peninsula and Points South

How far you drive down the Peninsula will depend on your time and special interests. If you're fascinated by Egyptology, you'll go all the way to San Jose, where the **Rosicrucian Egyptian Museum and Planetarium** (Park Avenue between Naglee and Randol; 408/947-3636) is located. The Egyptian artifacts on display include mummies, sculpture, jewelry, and objects important to everyday life. There's a replica of an Egyptian tomb and also a contemporary art gallery, in addition to collections of Babylonian, Assyrian, and Sumerian archaeological objects. The museum is open daily 9 A.M. to 5 P.M. (Phone for planetarium and science center show schedules. Admission is $6 for adults, $3.50 for students and people over 65, and $3 for children 7 to 15.)

Amateur astronomers won't want to miss **Lick Observatory,** nineteen miles east of San Jose on the 4,209-foot summit of Mount Hamilton (408/274-5061). The observatory, now an observation station, was established in 1876. Free tours of the main building are offered daily, 12:30 to 5 P.M. A visitors gallery at the location of the 120-inch telescope is open 10 A.M. to 5 P.M.

Though admission is fairly hefty ($12.50 for adults; $9.50 for people over 64; $6.50 for children 6 to 12), you may want to take in the **Winchester Mystery House** (525 S. Winchester Boulevard; 408/247-2101), the bizarre 160-room mansion designed by Sarah Winchester to confuse the evil spirits that haunted her. The eccentric heiress to the Winchester arms fortune and her servants needed maps to find their way around the house, which contains two thousand doors, secret passageways, ten thousand windows, and staircases leading nowhere. Guided tours of the mansion last a little more than an hour, and self-guiding tour maps of the grounds are available. The mansion is open daily in summer, 9 A.M. to 8 P.M.; in fall and spring Monday through Friday, 9 A.M. to 4:30 P.M.; and Saturday and Sunday, 9 A.M. to 5 P.M.

If you want to experience shopping and education at their

upscale best closer to San Francisco, stroll around the Stanford Shopping Center off El Camino Real on the south edge of Menlo Park. Then drive a few blocks farther south, turn right, and you'll be on the impressive Palm Drive leading to **Stanford University.** The sandstone buildings of the Stanford Quad (short for Quadrangle) shelter a courtyard that on sunny days with blue skies and essence of orange blossoms in the air is idyllic. Free guided tours of the campus are available.

Another charming spot in the Menlo Park–Stanford orbit is the **Allied Arts Guild** (75 Arbor Road; 415/325-3259) a cluster of shops and a lunchroom housed in Spanish-style buildings on property that was once part of the vast Rancho de las Pulgas, a land grant from the King of Spain. Visitors who like to drive around admiring the cream of country estates will find them in the communities of Atherton, Hillsborough, and Woodside.

The trip south of San Francisco is to the **Monterey Peninsula.** Though it's only 115 miles between San Francisco and Monterey, plan on at least four hours for the drive, as there are so many stops and detours you might want to make along the way. If you choose to travel Highway 1, the coastal route, your first stop may well be **Half Moon Bay,** a rustic community with small-town buildings and old-fashioned streetlamps, or at **Princeton,** where most of the original fishing harbor lunchrooms have given way to tonier seafood restaurants.

This part of the coast is where middle-school science teachers take their students on field trips to study tide pool life. If you decide to do some tide pooling, beware of both the tides and the spiney urchins.

Farther down the coast is Ano Nuevo State Park—a great place from which to watch sea lions—and Santa Cruz (see chapter 10, Family Planning).

If you drive to the Monterey Peninsula on the inland Highway 101 and can't resist a bargain, you'll want to stop at **Horizon Outlet Center** (408/842-3729) in Gilroy (it's right next to the highway. With more than 150 outlet stores, it has the reputation among discount shoppers of being the best of its kind in Northern California.

Depending on which route you take, other stops might be outside of Watsonville at **Elkhorn Slough Natural Estuarine Research Reserve** (east of Highway 1 off the Dolan Road exit; 408/728-2822). It's the habitat of hundreds of species of birds, fish, and invertebrates, and one of the few relatively undisturbed wetlands remaining in California. Guided walks, which originate at the visitor center, are conducted Saturday and Sunday at 10 A.M. and 1 P.M. The reserve is open Wednesday through Sunday from 9 A.M. to 5 P.M. Admission is $2.50 for adults and free for people under the age of 16.

An important stop for people interested in California history or architecture is at **Mission San Juan Bautista** (2nd and Mariposa streets, San Juan Bautista; 408/623-4881). Largest of the mission churches, it is the only one with a three-aisle entrance to the altar. The mission contains period furnishings, and its convent wing, with a collection of ecclesiastical objects, is especially interesting. Open daily, 9:30 A.M. to 4:30 P.M.; admission is free.

Surrounded by Monterey Bay to the north, the Pacific Ocean to the west and Carmel Bay to the south, the Monterey Peninsula contains some of the most glorious—and most photographed—real estate on earth.

There are three major population centers on the peninsula—Monterey, Pacific Grove, and Carmel—each with its own character. And though it's only four miles between Monterey and Carmel on Highway 1, most visitors choose to go the long way via the famous **Seventeen-Mile Drive.**

Not only is the area scenically a wow, it's historically one of California's most interesting spots—Monterey served as the capital of both Alta (Upper) and Baja (Lower) California at one time during the Spanish colonial era. The peninsula's Spanish and Mexican heritage dates back to 1602, when Sebastian Vizcaino sailed into Monterey Harbor. And though you'll find historic sites, such as the Carmel Mission, on other parts of the Monterey Peninsula, it's in the City of Monterey where you'll find most of the tangible evidence of the area's early history.

Royal Presidio Chapel (550 Church Street), the oldest structure, was built in 1794 and has been in continuous operation ever since. Other important buildings include **Colton Hall** on Pacific Street (408/646-5640) where the first California constitution was written, in 1849, and **Casa Sobranes** (336 Pacific Street), occupied by the Sobranes family from 1840 to 1922. The **custom house** on Custom House Plaza is the oldest government building in California, with one section dating back to 1827.

Maps for a two-mile "Monterey Path of History" walking tour, which passes by adobes, historic sites, and some lovely gardens, are available at the visitor center (204 Camino El Estero) and the **Monterey Peninsula Chamber of Commerce** (380 Alvarado Street, Monterey; 408/649-1770).

Ideal for a long hike—or a short stroll—the eighteen-mile **Monterey Peninsula Recreation Trail** stretches from the city of Castroville, "Artichoke Capital of the World," to Asilomar State Beach in Pacific Grove. The integrated cycling and pedestrian path, formerly a Southern Pacific Railroad right-of-way, gives the public access to some of California's most scenic coastal areas and passes by many of the area's points of interest.

Monterey Bay Aquarium (886 Cannery Row; 408/648-4888), home to more than 6,500 creatures of the sea, is one of the great aquariums of the world, if not the absolute best. More than five hundred species of marine life live in twenty-three major habitat areas. There's a two-story sea otter exhibit and a kelp forest three stories high. A series of smaller tanks contain kaleidoscopes of angelfish, soldierfish, butterflyfish, parrotfish, and dozens of other varieties.

The new Outer Bay galleries are the first in the world to present life in the open ocean on a grand scale. This one-million-gallon exhibit showcases the waters where Monterey

IN THE STEPS OF STEINBECK

Author John Steinbeck called Monterey's **Cannery Row** "a poem, a stink, a grating noise, a quality of light, a tone, a habit, a nostalgia, a dream." Today, the stink of sardines is gone from the Row, and the noise of the canning machinery has been replaced by that of traffic and tourist voices. But the buildings Steinbeck immortalized in his 1945 novel *Cannery Row* are still there—some of them renovated—housing more than a hundred specialty shops and restaurants. However, it is still possible to identify some of Steinbeck's sites.

The weather-beaten lab at 800 Cannery Row served as Ed "Doc" Rickett's base of operations when he wasn't off hunting for marine specimens for area laboratories. Lee Chong's Heavenly Flower Grocery is now an antique shop. La Ida, where "understudy" bartender Eddie collected patrons' unfinished drinks in a jug to take back to his friends at the Palace Flophouse and Grill, is now occupied by a restaurant. The fictional Chin Kee's Squid Yard in *Cannery Row*'s sequel, *Sweet Thursday,* was located where Hopkins Marine Station now stands.

Many of the places that inspired Steinbeck's fictional settings for his other books, such as *East of Eden,* are in Salinas, where the author was born. Also in Salinas—eighteen miles from Monterey—are the **Steinbeck Center Foundation** (408/753-6411) and the **John Steinbeck Public Library** (350 Lincoln Avenue; 408/758-7311), where a special room is devoted to his works and the house where he grew up.

Bay meets the Pacific Ocean and is the dwelling place oɪ soupfin sharks, green sea turtles, barracuda, and ocean sunfish that can grow to ten feet and weigh three thousand pounds. Visitors view Outer Bay through the largest window in the world, an acrylic panel fifteen feet high and fifty-four feet long, weighing seventy-eight thousand pounds.

There are fish feedings in various parts of the aquarium,

and in the afternoon, live video transmissions from a research submarine in Monterey Bay at depths of six thousand feet. (Open daily except Christmas, 10 A.M. to 6 P.M. It opens at 9 A.M. June 20 to Labor Day; admission is $13.75 for adults; $11.75 for people 13 to 18 years and over 65; $6 for children 3 to 12 and the disabled.

Originally a pier where trading schooners unloaded and took on cargo, **Monterey's Fisherman's Wharf** is now a wood-planked promenade flanked by restaurants, small shops, and fish markets. It is also the place where sport fishing, sight-seeing, and whale-watching boats dock and a good place from which to watch seals, sea lions, and otters. The commercial fleet is now based at the Municipal Wharf, a few blocks away.

Parking is a problem in Monterey but not such a big one if you get the free "Smart Parking in Monterey" brochure, which explains parking laws and includes a map indicating the location of the thirty-three parking facilities operated by the city. Brochures are available at the Monterey Visitor Center (401 Camino El Estero) or by phoning the Monterey Peninsula Visitors and Convention Bureau (408/648-5373).

Most of the peninsula's hotel and motel rooms are located in Monterey and are almost as high priced as those in San Francisco. However, there are promotions and packages. For example, in the fall of 1996, the **Holiday Inn Resort Monterey** (1000 Aguajito Road; 800/234-5697; rack rates $115 to $160) advertised a "Monterey Bay Aquarium" package that featured a double room, breakfast for two, and two tickets to the aquarium for $119 ($10 additional on Friday and Saturday). Since the two tickets would cost $27.50, and most breakfasts for two go from $10 to $15, this represented savings of more than 30 percent off the lowest rate.

Special hotel and motel rates are frequently advertised in magazines such as *VIA*, the publication sent to members of the California Automobile Association.

As far as food is concerned, if ever there was a place for

picnics, the Monterey Peninsula is it. Wherever you go, there's a rock or a bench to sit on and something fabulous to look at. Even if it's windy and you have to eat in the car, you can still feast your eyes on the scenery.

Area strawberries, olallieberries, vine-ripe tomatoes, and fresh fruit are all available at country stands in season. Cracked crab and other seafood are fresh at Fisherman's Wharf.

In general, restaurants are geared to the tourist trade, and it's easy to get an overpriced, ho-hum meal. However, there are exceptions. For instance, if you want to pull out all the stops, **Fresh Cream** is expensive (most entrées are $26 or less), but the food and ambience are outstanding (100C Heritage Harbor; 408/375-9798).

The **Monterey Wine Country** is the third largest fine wine producing region in the United States, and you can sample wines from thirty of the wineries at **A Taste of Monterey** (700 Cannery Row; 408/646-5446) while looking through a windowed wall at the entire Monterey Bay. Tasting costs $2 for three wines; $3 for six. Snacks featuring local products (grilled artichokes, roasted garlic, smoked salmon, veggies with ranch dressing, and cheese with crackers) cost from $3 to $8, so time your visit to make it a lunch or early dinner stop.

Adjacent to Monterey to the northwest, **Pacific Grove** is best known for the hundreds of thousands of monarch butterflies that winter there from mid-October to mid-February each year. They congregate in clusters at two places in town— in Washington Park along a trail beginning at Spruce and Alder streets, and at the Monarch Grove Sanctuary, just off Lighthouse Avenue at Ridge Road. Look, but don't touch— there's a 1939 city ordinance that authorizes a $500 fine for anyone caught "molesting a butterfly in any way."

If your visit doesn't coincide with the monarchs', you can still learn a good deal about them at the monarch butterfly display of the **Pacific Grove Museum of Natural History** (corner of Forest and Central avenues; 408/648-3117). There's also a video that chronicles the monarch's metamorphosis and a gift shop featuring butterfly-related items.

The bed and breakfast establishments along Pacific Grove's Oceanview Boulevard are ideal places to stay for people who want to be within walking distance of the aquarium and Cannery Row, yet have less crowded walkways along the bay just across the street. One of the nicest is **Martine Inn** (255 Oceanview Boulevard; 408/373-3388 or 800/852-5588). Rates in this beautifully furnished, Mediterranean-style property go from $125 to $230 and include a full breakfast, with wine and hors d'oeuvres in the early evening, and free on-site parking. Other Pacific Grove lodging standouts are the **Green Gables Inn** and the **Gosby House Inn** (see chapter 2, Bedtime Bargains).

The Seventeen-Mile Drive tollgates in Pacific Grove signal the beginning of one of the most impressive drives in the world, and not only because of its natural splendor. The posh homes and resorts are awesome, too. The drive is also famous for its **golf layouts.** The top courses—Spyglass Hill, Pebble Beach, and Cypress Point—are consistently rated among the top ten courses internationally and are where many prestigious tournaments take place.

When there isn't a tournament going on, you can play the course—for a price. Pebble Beach Golf Links costs $225 plus cart rental for eighteen holes. Spyglass is $175 plus cart rental, and the Inn at Spanish Bay is a mere $145 excluding cart fee. But though it costs a mint to play the courses, it doesn't cost a cent to stop at the Inn at Spanish Bay or the Lodge at Pebble Beach to stretch your legs, admire the view, and soak up the ambience.

If you're like most visitors, bring along plenty of film and food on your drive, because you'll want to stop often to take photos, and the fresh air is bound to make you hungry.

At the other end of the Seventeen-Mile Drive, **Carmel-by-the-Sea** was established in 1905 by a group of artists and writers enthralled by its idyllic setting. Residential areas are a mix of styles with charming effect—a Swiss chalet, a house designed like the captain's quarters on a ship, a French country home with mansard roof, an American-style cottage from the 1920s.

Downtown is crammed with quaint buildings, beautiful plantings, specialty stores, and tourists. Though poking about for an hour or two is fun, the process is fatiguing by late morning, when crowds begin to arrive. You'll probably enjoy your visit more if you wander the residential streets or walk beside the ocean, soaking up the same atmosphere the artists discovered almost a century ago.

The best times to visit the Monterey Peninsula are in the spring and fall. Winter brings rain, and summer mornings are often fogged in. But any time is better than missing the trip because the weather isn't perfect.

CHAPTER

13

Sources and Resources

People don't usually get the good San Francisco deals just because they're lucky. It takes some time and a bit of effort to consistently get top value for the money you spend. Some of the information you need, such as that to make airfare or room-rate comparisons, can be found by calling toll-free numbers. General information on San Francisco accommodations, attractions, sight-seeing, and special events is available from:

> San Francisco Convention and Visitors Bureau
> 201 Third Street
> San Francisco, CA 94103
> 415/391-2000 (French, 391-2003; German, 391-2004;
>   Spanish, 391-2122; and Japanese, 391-2101)

The more specific you are about your requirements and interests, the better the people who receive your letters will be able to provide the information you need. Expect to pay a nominal fee for some of the printed information and brochures you receive from the convention and visitors bureau.

When you arrive in The City, one of the first stops should be the visitor center on the lower level of **Hallidie Plaza** at the corner of Powell and Market Streets. The multilingual staff will answer any questions you might have, and the racks are full of brochures, many of them containing discount coupons.

You may also want to send for sample copies of the free

magazines that are available at hotels and the visitor center. When you order a single issue, however, you may be charged as much as $4.

Bay City Guide
Guide Publishing Group, Inc.
455 North Point
San Francisco, CA 94133
415/929-7722
website at http://www.sfousa.com

FYI
520 Hampshire Street
San Francisco, CA 94110
415/225-3100
E-mail: fyisf@sfbayguardian.com

Key
L. Publishing, Inc.
1164 Bryant Street
San Francisco, CA 94103
415/865-2300

San Francisco Guide
2087 Union Street, Suite 1
San Francisco, CA 94123
415/775-2212
(For mailed copies, send $2 for postage and handling.)

San Francisco Quick Guide
220 Montgomery Street, Suite 994
San Francisco, CA 94101
415/362-8384

Where
74 New Montgomery Street, Suite 320
San Francisco, CA 94105
415/546-6101
website at http://www.wheremags.com/world
($4, single issue; $18, twelve issues)

It also could be worth your while to subscribe to the *San Francisco Examiner*'s Sunday edition for a few weeks in advance of your visit (415/777-7800 is the circulation department number).

If you travel a good deal, it might be a smart financial move to subscribe to Consumer Reports Travel Letter (Subscription Department, P.O. Box 51366, Boulder, CO 80323). The newsletter alerts readers to charge-card travel benefits, tells them how to spot travel scams, and shows, with examples, ways to get the best deals in airfares, hotel rooms, car rentals, and restaurant meals. A one-year (twelve-issue) subscription costs $39.

Although there are some good maps in "The San Francisco Book," the informational booklet distributed by the San Francisco Convention and Visitors Bureau, you may want to invest in Flashmaps ($8.95 at bookstores). With seating diagrams of ballparks and theaters, separate maps locating restaurants, museums, attractions, and a number of other sites by category, it can be a very useful addition to your travel information packet. For a bus and ferry system map, contact:

> Golden Gate Transit
> Box 9000
> Presidio Station
> San Francisco, CA 94129

You can also get ferry schedule and rate information by telephoning 415/923-2000.

Transportation

A brochure listing Bay Area Rapid Transit schedules, fares, and general information is published by:

> BART
> 800 Madison
> Oakland, CA
> 510/464-6000

Information on the San Francisco Municipal Railway system (buses, cable cars, and streetcars) is available from:

San Francisco Municipal Railway
949 Presidio Avenue
San Francisco, CA 94115
415/923-6142

The municipal railway also publishes a brochure called the "Muni Access Guide" that tells about the bus and light rail services that can accommodate the disabled.

"The Bicycle Rider Directory" ($3.95) is an excellent guide that includes information on cycling along the California coast north of San Francisco, on Angel Island, in the East Bay, from Santa Cruz to San Francisco, as well as in the Napa and Sonoma valleys. Maps indicate bike paths, good biking roads, no-biking roads, and roads on which riders must be attentive. In addition to the bicycle paths, many of the off-highway roads in the valleys are great for bicycling, with little traffic and picturesque views wherever you look.

Accommodations

A guide listing hotels and motels by area is available from the San Francisco Convention and Visitors Bureau. It's also a good idea to contact directly the hotels that interest you, requesting rate sheets, brochures, and information on any special promotions.

Dining

Libraries often have back copy files of major metropolitan newspapers. They are an excellent source for restaurant reviews that are usually fairly objective and unbiased.

Seniors

For complete information on Elderhostel contact:

Elderhostel
75 Federal Street
Boston, MA 02110

Day Trips and Excursions

When planning any day trip or excursion, it's good to get all the information you can in advance, and the entities promoting tourism in their areas are usually prompt in sending it to you. If you're interested in specifics, such as riding stables or gold-panning operations, mention them. The following are organizations representing the destinations showcased in this book, with the addition of others in areas that might interest you.

Amador County Chamber of Commerce
125 Peek Avenue, Suite B
Jackson, CA 95642
209/233-0350

Belvedere-Tiburon Chamber of Commerce
96-B Main Street
Tiburon, CA 94920
415/435-5633

Benecia Chamber of Commerce
601 1st Street
Benecia, CA 94510
707/745-2120

Berkeley Convention and Visitors Bureau
1834 University Avenue, 1st floor
Berkeley, CA 94703
510/549-7040

Calistoga Chamber of Commerce
Old Depot Building, Lincoln Avenue
Calistoga, CA (94515)
707/942-6333

El Dorado County Chamber of Commerce
542 Main Street
Placerville, CA 95667
916/621-5885

Fort Bragg–Mendocino Coast Chamber of Commerce
322 N. Main Street
Fort Bragg, CA 95437
707/961-6300 or 800/726-2780

John Steinbeck Library
110 W. San Luis Street
Salinas, CA 93906
408/758-7311

Lake Tahoe Visitors Authority
1156 Ski Run Boulevard
South Lake Tahoe, CA 96150
916/544-5050

Larkspur Chamber of Commerce
P.O. Box 315
Larkspur, CA 94993
415/257-8338

Monterey Peninsula Visitors and Convention Bureau
P.O. Box 1770
Monterey, CA 93942
408/649-1770 (visitor information)

National Maritime Museum Association
Building 35, Fort Mason
San Francisco, CA 94114
415/929-0202

National Park Service
Point Reyes National Seashore
Point Reyes Station, CA 94956
415/633-1092 (Bear Valley Visitor Center)

Nevada City Chamber of Commerce
132 Main Street
Nevada City, CA 95959
916/265-2692

North Lake Tahoe Resort Association
P.O. Box 5578
Tahoe City, CA 96145
916/583-3494 or 800/824-6348

Oakland Convention and Visitors Bureau
1000 Broadway, Suite 200
Oakland, CA 94607
510/839-9000

Palo Alto Chamber of Commerce
325 Forest Avenue
Palo Alto, CA 94302
415/324-3121

Sacramento Convention and Visitors Bureau
1421 K Street
Sacramento, CA 95814
916/264-7777

St. Helena Chamber of Commerce
1020 Main Street
St. Helena, CA 94574
707/963-4456

San Jose Convention and Visitors Bureau
333 W. San Carlos Street, Suite 1000
San Jose, CA 95110
408/295-9600

Santa Cruz Chamber of Commerce
1543 Pacific Avenue
Santa Cruz, CA 95060
408/423-1111

Sausalito Chamber of Commerce
333 Caledonia Street
Sausalito, CA 94965
415/331-7262
(Sausalito Visitor Center phone is 415/332-0505)

Sonoma Valley Chamber of Commerce
645 Broadway
Sonoma, CA 95476
707/996-1033

Steinbeck Center Foundation
Salinas, CA (currently under construction)
408/753-6411

Tuolumne County Visitors Bureau
55 Stockton Street
Sonora, CA 95370
209/533-4420 or 800/446-1332

West Marin Chamber of Commerce
11431 California Highway 1, no. 17
Point Reyes Station, CA 94956
415/472-7470

Yountville Chamber of Commerce
6416 Yount Street
Yountville, CA 94599
707/944-0904

For detailed information on what events are taking place in California to commemorate the 150-year anniversaries of the discovery of gold and statehood, write to:

California Gold Discovery to Statehood
   Sesquicentennial
914 Capitol Mall, Suite 217
Sacramento, CA 95814